CAT & NAT'S

# Mom
# Secrets

Also by Catherine Belknap and Natalie Telfer

*Cat and Nat's Mom Truths: Embarrassing Stories and Brutally Honest Advice on the Extremely Real Struggle of Motherhood*

CAT & NAT'S

# Mom Secrets

Coffee-Fueled Confessions from the Mom Trenches

## CATHERINE BELKNAP
## NATALIE TELFER

RODALE BOOKS
NEW YORK

Published in the United States by Rodale Books, an imprint of Random House,
a division of Penguin Random House LLC, New York.
rodalebooks.com

RODALE and the Plant colophon are registered trademarks
of Penguin Random House LLC.

Library of Congress Cataloging-in-Publication Data
Names: Belknap, Catherine, author. | Telfer, Natalie, author.
Title: Cat and Nat's mom secrets : coffee-fueled confessions from the mom trenches /
Catherine Belknap, Natalie Telfer.
Other titles: Mom secrets
Description: First edition. | New York : Rodale Books, 2022.
Identifiers: LCCN 2021053930 (print) | LCCN 2021053931 (ebook) |
ISBN 9780593139295 (trade paperback) | ISBN 9780593139301 (ebook)
Subjects: LCSH: Motherhood. | Motherhood—Humor.
Classification: LCC HQ759 .B4447 2022  (print) | LCC HQ759  (ebook) |
DDC 306.874/3—dc23/eng/20211223
LC record available at https://lccn.loc.gov/2021053930
LC ebook record available at https://lccn.loc.gov/2021053931

ISBN 978-0-593-13929-5
Ebook ISBN 978-0-593-13930-1

Printed in the United States of America

Editor: Donna Lofreddo
Editorial Assistant: Katherine Leak
Art Directors: Jennifer K. Beal Davis and Anna Bauer
Illustrations: Lana Le
Designer: Jen Valero
Cover Design: Lynn Buckley
Production Manager: Kelli Tokos
Production Editor: Terry Deal
Composition: Scribe
Copy Editor: Ivy K. McFadden
Marketer: Tammy Blake
Publicist: Ray Arjune

1st Printing

First Edition

To our husbands, our children, and all the people who have shared their secrets with us

# CONTENTS

# ONE

# 500-Seat Confession Booth

*t's the kind of moment that feels like a dream.* I'm backstage, in a different country, with my best friend in the world, Cat, about to put on the very first show of a business we've created together. It's all I can think as I hear the crowd just meters away, on the other side of the curtain, give a loud cheer. They roar. The music thrums, the lights sparkle. Time seems to pause, and a supercut of the months leading up to this moment flashes in my mind. Endless phone calls, family strategizing, text threads with Cat, freezing meals, planning playdates, talking to our team, coordinating carpools, business meetings, day planners full of schedule shifts.

And now, here we are. At the Tobin Center in San Antonio, mere moments and steps away from hundreds of fans who have come here for *us*. For us, and for themselves. To be swept away by a night of glitz and laughs. To make us a part of their real lives—not just their idle scrolling. And I want to make this night the perfect escape for them, an escape from their own endless text threads planning playdates and day planners full of scheduling mathematics worthy of NASA.

Suddenly, it seems almost ridiculous. We have no script. We're just two moms who make each other laugh. What if it doesn't translate to the big stage? My body revolts against me. Palms sweating, heart quickening in time with the rising beat of the DJ, breath getting tight, legs unsteady. This feels like more than stage fright. It's panic, the disastrous possibility of letting these people in the audience down. They arranged babysitters for this. We need to make it worth the babysitters' fees and the guilt for taking a night off from their kids. Can we do this? I feel dizzy.

I turn to grab Cat's hand. As I try to mouth *HELP*, which my tense muscles can barely manage to articulate, she breaks into a huge, face-splitting grin.

"I'M DRUNK!" she says, laughing and glittering.

For most people, this would be the final straw that turns a near breakdown to a full-on panic attack. But it's me, and it's Cat. Seeing her laugh gleefully and mischievously, without a care in the world, put me right back into the spirit of this thing. We were here to take *away* feelings of nerves, guilt, anxiety, and stress. We were here to alleviate all the things that make women, mothers, and parents feel not good enough. We were here to be *ourselves*— that's what these people came for! Who knows why, but they want our messy, beautiful, silly, inappropriate, wild—and, apparently, drunk—selves. We've never promised to be perfect—or even sober, I guess. We're just them, with microphones.

The beginning of our intro song starts to play, and my insides swell with anticipation. It's showtime. And this show did have quite an unexpected twist to it, but not at all in the way we expected.

But before we go any further, let us tell you about how we got to that moment in the first place.

After grueling preparations to make sure our families survived our absence, Cat and I are sitting pretty. More specifically, sitting pretty on a plane, Texas-bound for the first leg of our multi-city tour, and eagerly signaling the flight attendant over for some beverages. We're reeling from the fact that hundreds of people have paid real, actual money to see us live, but relieved we made our flight at all. Finally, we let out a sigh of relief. All the planning has paid off, and now it's just time to carry out those plans. On theme with our first stop, we order some tequila cocktails to celebrate.

Unfortunately, we opted for the extravagantly expensive in-flight Wi-Fi—one of those inventions you think is going to make your life so much better, but actually makes it so much worse. You're supposed to be unavailable for those glorious hours on a plane! Who allowed that to change! A few sips in, we decide we should post some fun pre-show, en-route pictures on our social media to get our fans excited for the tour.

But the internet giveth and the internet taketh away.

Across the aisle, our beloved Sam, tour team leader, is also connecting to Wi-Fi. She gives us a pained look, and at first we think it's just because she spent the past half hour puking into a paper bag (eight weeks pregnant, unbeknownst to us), but then we realize it's more than sickness.

"Gals, I just got an email," she says. "Our whole team of male strippers have come down with the flu."

This was pre-COVID, so the flu qualified as a major disaster. We never expected smooth sailing (after all, it's *us*), but we'd already lost out on the hottest DJ in Texas—some shirtless cowboy who was booked until next century—and had to replace him with a wedding DJ our sweet assistant booked because he "sounded nice."

We order another round of drinks—not celebration drinks this time . . . nerve-calming drinks. Please-God-let-us-find-hot-guys-to-dance-for-the-moms drinks.

We open up our laptops and start frantically googling. I type in "last minute hot male strippers" and see Cat type "emergency hot guys for rent." We're trying everything we can: "24/7 men dancers," "strippers available TONIGHT SAN ANTONIO HELP." Because we *need* the hot strippers. A cardboard cutout of Channing Tatum just won't do. (How does one get one of those hologram projectors they use to bring back dead celebrities?) No. We promised hundreds of moms living, breathing, gyrating, and, above all, hot strippers. They juggled their schedules, booked babysitters, meal-prepped, got dressed up, and paid for Ubers for this. We are not going to let them down, no matter how bleak the options for no-notice San Antonio hotties looks.

We land in Texas, and our team has decided we should do a little sightseeing to get a feel for the area before the show tonight. But all we can think about is hot half-naked men and it's making us miserable. Finally, we get word that someone knows someone who knows someone else who has a hookup for replacement strippers. Beggars can't be choosers, so we're like, "Okay, good enough for us!"

We have to get started on our pre-show routine, you see. Like a diva trilling through multiple octaves before hitting the stage, Cat and I need to warm up our instrument. Our art is riffing and joking, so that's what we need to do. We hit the town, checking out the shops, sampling the local beverages, chatting about things we can bring up during the show. This is our rehearsal for the off-the-cuff style that is our bread and butter. Three-minute YouTube videos in our parked SUVs, three-hour live show in front of an audience, what's the difference?

We soak up the sights, and soak up some more alcohol, too. I am liking business trips more with each margarita. When we arrive at the venue, women are lined up around the block already. It's exactly what we dreamed of—these hot mamas laughing, chatting, meeting each other. The energy is contagious, and we rush inside to freshen our makeup and get our show outfits on.

An hour before showtime, we meet the DJ. He is indeed, uh, *nice*. But he seems like he'd be more at home at a library than on a stage in front of screaming moms who have escaped their homes and families for a precious night out.

"At least our dancers will spice things up a little," Cat whispers to me. And just then, our scantily clad troupe saunters down the hall toward us for introduction.

"Oh my God," I whisper-scream in Cat's ear. "Did we hire high-schoolers by accident?!"

Our Chippendales were looking more like Chip 'n' Dale. Cat and I look at each other. Okay, okay, not to worry. Men aren't the main draw of this event anyway! Nope, not about men at all—this is about divine feminine bonding, I think with desperation. And the stage adds ten years, right? They're meant to be accessories to our jokes and games . . . and how bad can they be, really?

Now we're back where we started this story: onstage. We're trying not to die of secondhand embarrassment as the scrawny, dirty-jeaned strippers we're subjecting this audience to are doing their "routine": moves that bring us flashbacks of sweaty adolescent school-dance thrusting. Cat can see in my eyes that I'm starting to panic, so she cues the DJ to turn down the music and we transition into the Q&A section of the evening. I worry that we might be losing the crowd; this isn't the sexy little night out they'd envisioned. Mics are passed into the audience.

A woman who appears to be here alone stands to take the mic. The crowd hushes. She speaks clearly, though she seems shy. She introduces herself and says, "I'm a single mom trying to be both a mother and a father to my kids, and every day I feel like I'm failing them. All around me I see groups of friends and moms who came with their besties, but I don't have mom friends. I wish I had my own Cat to my Nat to walk with me through life."

It's quiet for the first time since the show started. My heart aches for this woman. Though I'm not a single mom, and I'm the Nat to the Cat, I still relate to what she's said. I look to Cat, wondering how we should answer this woman who has not so much asked us a question, but bared a really vulnerable part of herself. Thankfully, our beautiful community picks up on our pause.

A woman across the audience stands up and says, "I'm a single mom, too, and I feel the exact same way. You're not alone."

One after another, women chime in in agreement—they too feel alone, like they don't have what they want, that connection, to feel seen and to feel they're part of a community. They feel isolated, they don't have it all figured out. Through these admissions, through the bravery it takes to actually *say* that you're lonely to hundreds of people, they have created a bridge toward each other. It's an emotional moment. Cat and I look at each other with tears in our eyes. This night isn't about strippers or cocktails or glitzy dresses after all. It's about creating the space for fun and vulnerability to exist simultaneously, so that people feel comfortable enough to show the not-so-Instagrammable versions of themselves. This is a place where women can be real with each other. They can find community and support one another—and also have a little fun. A shared laugh can go a long way.

In the end, the night turned out to be a blueprint for how we would run the show going forward. We'd still stand backstage in jittery anticipation for a show with high energy, high expectations, and no script (although we have since upgraded our dancers to ones of legal drinking age). And beyond bonding over letting our hair down, shaking off the crumbs, stains, and snot of our kids, getting a few good drinks in us, and dancing together, what our show is really about is making other mothers feel less alone.

That first mom who took the mic and got vulnerable with us inspired us to make a regular segment of our live shows: Mom Confessions. We do this because we've received enough DMs and emails to know that moms all over the world can feel selfish, mean, unorganized, irresponsible just because they aren't the 100% flawless perfect mother they feel they're expected to be. But there is no such thing as the perfect mother. We hope that in having a place to confess these feelings, we can banish stigmas, inject a little humor to relieve some stress, and realize that the shortcomings we think are ours alone are actually shared by *so many others*. No matter where you live, no matter what your socioeconomic status, ethnicity, age, race, or education, moms share more in common with one another than we realize. Motherhood, like many good things in life, is full of contradictions: it is the most frustrating, heart-wrenching, difficult, and isolating role, and it's also the most wonderful, rewarding, inspiring, fun, and unifying.

So we have to thank those San Antonio strippers who canceled on us after getting the flu. If not for them, we might not have opened up that Q&A, and that woman might have left the show still feeling isolated.

We've written this book as an extension of the Mom Confessions segment of our shows. Though it may not include a cash bar, please, by all means, put on some party music and pour yourself your drink of choice. In this book, you'll find confessions of every variety from women all around the world, with responses from us, Cat and Nat. And we hope you know that we're speaking directly to *you*, from our hearts and our experiences. Whether you already have your mom community or are in search of one—look no further. We got you. And we hope that this book will make you laugh, give you comfort, and remind you that we are really, really all on this wild ride of motherhood together.

# TWO

# *The Bachelor— But with Your Kids*

**Confession:** *"This one mom at school is always Facebook posting about these one-on-one activities she goes on with each of her kids, preaching how incredible they are and how noticed her kids feel. Am I a bad parent for not taking the time to do this kind of thing?" –Anonymous*

Every year, television proves there is an insatiable appetite for dating shows. From our favorite, *Love Island*, to increasingly bizarre premises that seem more like twisted psychological experiments, clearly we can't get enough of hot strangers getting it on. (Hey, ABC, we have your next idea: A naive couple gets married and has kids and then they never see or speak to each other until their thirtieth anniversary when—if they've made it this far—they get to go to a sexy island getaway. Sure, the twenty-eight seasons in the middle might be a little slow, but the finale will include a candlelit seaside dinner and an argument brought on by three too many mai tais. Call us if you want to talk logistics.)

But long before the gimmicky spin-offs, there was the classic, the original: *The Bachelor*. One hot gentleman whittling down a slew of gorgeous ladies—who, if they play their cards right, can turn a breathless "Can I steal you for a sec?" into one-on-ones involving bungee jumping and (kind of awkward) private concerts later in the season. We love to watch the drama unfold from the comfort of our couches, but the one place we didn't expect it to materialize would be in our real lives as parents.

From mommy bloggers to child psychologists, parenting advice from all over the world is now pushing a new responsibility: one-on-one time with your kids. More specifically, the concept of "dating your kids," taking them on fulfilling, creative one-on-ones to show them how special they are to you, and to check in with them.

Now, this is obviously wonderful in theory. Especially when you have multiple kids (as you might remember, I have three and Nat has four), making sure each one feels special, feels that they have a connection to you, and that you're paying attention to their needs is totally important. And theoretically, this one-on-one time could mean anything. But of course, in the new age of the Instagram-mom, special time has morphed into something that makes everyone else jealous. These are not your average parent-kid hangouts or special treats. We're not talking about reading a bedtime story, or rewatching *Frozen* for the seventeenth time on a Friday night, or letting them get a cake pop before making them sit and watch their sibling's soccer game for an hour. Of course not.

Much like *The Bachelor* one-on-ones, in order for these kid dates to be meaningful (or at least meaningful enough to brag about online), they seem to require not only the time to do the activity, but planning ahead, too. And we're expected to do this once a *month*?! I barely have time to get a wax once a month, or take my *husband* out for dinner once a month, let alone tote three/four different children to the new VR arcade downtown, or whatever other glitzy afternoons Instagram-moms are providing. It's way too much pressure.

I talked to Nat about it on the phone one night.

"I've been thinking about the 'dating your kids' thing again," I say to her.

"Oh God, here comes the guilt spiral."

"I know, I know. Why have we all become crazy internet moms who feel like we need to be going on dates with our kids to spend quality time with them?"

"Uh, because it looks better on Facebook?"

"I know. I keep seeing these long captions and photos like, hiking and skiing together, and I'm like, oh shit, I haven't even *thought* about hiking in years."

"Didn't your dad use to, like, rent a limo and take you to the CN Tower as a kid?" she says.

"Yeah," I say, "but that was like once every *two years*, not every month!"

"True. Plus, who needs to see the CN Tower once a month? Or even once ever? You go to the top, you look down . . . that's kinda it . . ."

"You know, Nat, some of these moms go away on *trips* together with their kids."

"Oh yeah, someone I know took her daughter to New York, so casually, to 'get some one-on-one time.' That's what she posted."

"A one-on-one vacation with your child?! I have a husband! I'm not trying to date my children, I'm trying to fucking *raise* them."

But social media is that cursed nightmare of a gift that keeps on giving. It plants this idea in my head like a parasite, slowly taking over my brain until I forget all about the last time I tried to do the one-on-one—when I took one of my kids for a date at Boston Pizza (children's menu plus alcohol menu, the two requirements) and then the other kids thought that was way cooler than where I took them. I promised them I'd take them all there next month. It's like I've lined my kids up *Bachelorette*-style and am giving them each a rose. "*You* get to go to the restaurant, and *you* get to go to the restaurant! Congratulations, kiddo, you've made it to the next week of this reality show we call parenting." Then I'm thinking about what a freak I'm going to look like to the waitstaff, showing up to this restaurant with three different children in the same month. But before that's even a possibility, life gets in the way. Come on, you really think I'm going to be able to take my kids out once a *week*? And that my husband can do the same? Three kids, two adults, seven days, that's not even logistically possible. But the Instagram parasite makes you forget all about that. Suddenly it's hanging over me, and I'm feeling so guilty all the time. If only I had the *Bachelor* production team and budget to just organize it all for me, and all I'd have to do is show up for my helicopter ride.

So the cycle begins: Nat and I will think about doing these one-on-one dates, swear we're going to do it. Try to have one-on-one time with each kid, once a week. Okay, fine, once a *month*. We do it for one month, and I'm feeling like the best mom on earth. Then someone's soccer practice changes schedule. Oh wait, and now my son needs homework help on the night I'm supposed to be going out with my daughter. My husband is running late from work. And obviously, no one has even *thought* about what to have for dinner. So the whole plan crumbles, and fuck it, we nix it. I let them use their iPad for an extra half an hour instead. You know, quality time.

Then one night, months later, I'm lying in bed scrolling next to my husband, and I just keep seeing posts about it. It's infectious, this trend. Are we supposed to keep taking our kids on these one-on-ones until the end of time? When do we ever get a *break*?! Are these moms being sponsored by some conglomerate that wants us to spend more money at those weird places where your kid can jump on diffcrent kinds of trampolines or something? How on earth do they have the time, money, and *energy* to bring each child individually to an indoor water park?! It's all over my feed: moms splitting souped-up ice cream sundaes with a kid, moms with their kids at live-action Disney plays, moms on a freaking run with their kids (I refuse to believe those photos are real). These moms will be posting a picture of their kid on Facebook with a huge caption about how much they love her, what a powerhouse she is, they're so proud of her—

Girl. Your kid isn't even on Facebook! She can't even read! Who is this for?!

As I drift off to sleep with an Instagram feed of overachieving moms playing on the back of my eyelids, I think, You know what, I'm as good as these moms! I'm cute with my kids, I love them, I can do this. We have fun together. I can give them each the one-on-one time they deserve. And maybe, I think, it doesn't have to be so lavish.

I start with my youngest daughter. She's been a little moody lately, I think maybe some one-on-one time with me would be good for her. I take her out of school early, which I thought she'd love, but she's pissed because there's some sort of cupcake bake sale happening that she's now missing, so we're instantly off to a shitty start. I tell the teacher it's for a medical appointment, but instantly regret it when she starts asking for details—is my daughter all right? Since when did teachers need to be so involved? Yes, she's all right, I think to myself, she's just in need of quality time, but I tell the teacher she has a weird rash, because don't kids always? I take her to a nearby coffee shop. I get my regular large coffee and realize that I'm here with my daughter at a very adult hipster coffee shop.

"What do you want, sweetie?" I ask her.

She shrugs. "Do they have cupcakes?" I ask the barista, who's a surly teen with a septum piercing my daughter can't stop staring at, touching her own nose as if imagining what it'd feel like. The barista sneers at the cupcake question and points to a case of baked goods with labels like "goat cheese focaccia" and "leek sundried tomato scone." Not exactly the stuff of my daughter's palate. I get her orange juice and silently curse myself for not taking her to McDonald's.

We sit down at a table. Honestly, it feels kind of weird to be sitting at a coffee shop with my sweet little daughter. I try asking her how she is, what's going on at school, what her and her friends have been up to. She responds like a five-year-old, all over the place with a manically detailed story that only half makes sense, punctuated by pauses with eyes glazed over, as if she's imagining all the cupcakes she's missing.

Riveting reality TV, this is not.

Once we get home, I ask her if she wants to go for a walk together.

"Mom," she says to me, "I've had a lot of you today. Can you give me some space?"

Ouch. That seals the deal. No more bending over backward for the one-on-ones. While other kids might be waiting patiently for their monthly time with their parents, ours are like, "Why are you looking at me? Am I in trouble? Can you mind your own business? I had PLANS today!"

Ultimately, experts say that ten minutes of alone time here and there with your kids is really what you need to give them that same boost of parental attention. It's not about a luxe weekend with them, it's not about giving them glamorous special treatment. Honestly, if your kid grows up getting lavish dates every week, they're going to grow up to be a dickbag. Sorry! It's just true! No one gets that kind of special treatment in real life. Unless you're a hot twenty-two-year-old on *The Bachelor*, which I hope to God none of my kids ever are.

To be real, Nat and I know when one of the children needs a little something extra. We are lucky in that working from home, we get to see them often throughout the day. But that's where spending an extra ten minutes chatting with them alone, or making dinner together, watching a movie—can go a really long way. If they're having a tough week at school, it doesn't mean they get to go on a trip to New York (who can even afford that?!). Life is never just about you, it's never going to be all about you. Not with friends, or work, or school. You need to be a part of a team, and to find your place within the team. Nobody's *so* important in a family that they need to be treated like a prince or princess every week; nobody's that important in the world! So really, at the end of the day, if there's anything we can take from *The Bachelor*, it's that group dates might be horrible on the show, but group dates with your family in real life—those are great.

# THREE

# Back to the Future of Parenting

**Confession:** *"Does anyone else remember when we weren't in constant communication with the entire world through our phones? I sometimes feel like I would kill to be a parent back then. Keeping up with technology and apps and social media . . . it's insane. I can't keep track of every new app or feature I need to monitor." –Anonymous*

Every generation faces different parenting challenges. Whether it's sociopolitical changes or horrible fashion trends (we have the pics to prove it), each decade and each era brings with it its own delightful cocktail of fresh challenges and societal bizarreness. I wonder how our parents would have reacted if we'd told them our kids would have these small, portable tools that give them 24/7 access to . . . all the knowledge known to man? (And yet they use them for TikTok.) At every point in time, information has flowed and connections have been made. But while our parents may have had to deal with us hogging the landline or passing an inappropriate note in class, we have to figure out this shit. Let's climb into the DeLorean and buckle up—we're taking you for a ride Back to the Future of Parenting. (Otherwise known as the horrifying science fiction plots playing out in our houses on a daily basis.)

## CAT

The setting: the present day futuristic Wild West. The scene: our houses. The camera pans first to the upstairs, where I'm taking a break, in the bathroom. I'm on the toilet, scrolling Instagram for a second of alone time, when suddenly, the door bursts open. A tiny human is holding a large flat screen in her palm, chattering away. She turns so that her back is to me, her camera facing both of us. My youngest daughter is vlogging me on the toilet. "Make sure to subscribe!" her little voice eerily chirps while I try to cover my pubic region. "What are you doing?!" I yell. She's acting like I'm not even here, though she's managed to get me in frame like a pro.

I can't tell if she's talking to someone live or recording, so I snatch the iPad from her hands, and she looks at me like I've just ruined her career selling hair vitamins on Instagram. Thankfully, she was just recording a video for her pretend vlogging channel. We don't let her post, but that doesn't stop her from blathering on idly as if thousands of people are breathlessly awaiting her next update about her skincare routine (a bar of Dove soap and clear ChapStick). When I was five, we were making Barbies act out dramatic fight scenes and gossip about each other and all kiss the one Ken doll we owned. In this new world, "playing" means pretending that you're a famous YouTuber. Either she's still too young to know about personal space, or she doesn't care about my personal space, but after I grab the iPad and somehow avoid tripping on my pants, which are around my ankles, she's like, "MOOOOM, I'm doing a video!"

I take this as an opportunity for a parenting lesson. I tell her there are certain things that are not appropriate to record. Certain things need to be private. I go through the basics of what you can and can't do while you're filming yourself. I never thought I'd need to tell my children that they can't broadcast me while I'm on the toilet, but that's the world I'm living in.

## NAT

The scene: my kitchen, happy family, home-cooked meal that I actually spent time on. We're all sitting at the table for a nice family dinner. We're talking like normal, saying all the sorts of things you only say when it's just family around: the intimate, private moments with your people. Like my youngest son describing the difference between vaginas and penises and me telling my husband to shut up. Then I see my older son's phone is on the table. I ask him to put it away—no phones at the dinner table. "Awh, Mom!" he says. "But Jacob's on FaceTime."

I can't believe this. He finds it appropriate to secretly have his friend tuned into dinner? Why would the friend even want to listen to me talk about my illegal double parking at school drop-off?! We talk about a lot of things in this house, things I don't necessarily need my kid's friends repeating to their parents. Back in the day of common courtesy, having your kid's friends over for dinner would be a bit of an occasion. You choose noncontroversial topics of conversation, you discipline the kids a bit differently, you make your five-year-old wear underwear. Suddenly, our kids are bringing their friends to dinner, but virtually and secretly?! Nuh-uh.

Later that night after dinner, I walk downstairs and put on my current favorite true crime podcast. Hm, weird, I can't hear the audio. Then, as if narrated by a voice-projecting ventriloquist, I hear the grisly descriptions of a recently found body coming from the kitchen. I walk in and my son is on his hoverboard, swerving around the kitchen, with my audio coming out of the speaker in his board. I sigh. Bluetooth is dangerous—now even *I'm* getting involved in these futuristic traps. Thank God I wasn't watching porn.

## CAT

Then there are certain technology foibles we need to make sure we can prevent. Both of us decided to let our older kids have cell phones when we realized they were getting to an age where they would want to be out in the world without us, and we wanted to give them some of that freedom. But at the same time, they're not independent yet—I need them to be able to call me if they need me, or if they were lost or in trouble. The problem with cell phones of course is that they're not just used for calling your mother. Which led us to the inevitable conversation for our tweens: nudes. In one way, technology was working to our favor here. We had the ultimate threat. We informed them of something we were able to set up (but tbh, barely understand) called THE CLOUD. We said okay, just so you know, all our phones are connected by this cloud. So anything you take a photo of gets automatically uploaded to the cloud, and goes on to everyone else's device in the family. So do not take a nude, or else it's going to all of us!

Back to my daughter live-vlogging me from the toilet: the thing for kids is that we need to teach them boundaries with technology.

They see their parents filming their birthdays, their day-to-day activities, and sharing their lives online with friends, family, and strangers. So it's fair if they sometimes, especially when they're younger, don't know where the boundaries are between what is appropriate to film or take photos of and what's off-limits. There are always incidents in middle school and high school these days where kids get caught filming things they shouldn't. A therapist we know has said that because this is the way kids communicate nowadays, they aren't clear on the boundaries until they're told explicitly what not to record. We drilled it into our kids: once something is sent out there in the world, whether it's a text or a video you post online, you can't get it back.

## NAT

So you're maybe thinking, where do we draw the line? There are so many ways for all this technology to go wrong. Why don't we just ban it outright and go back to the days of analog? Kids, cuddle up, we're all going to listen to a radio program! Or we can sit around and listen to a Bon Jovi record together! Maybe I can whip out my Cabbage Patch Kid!

What did people do before iPads? Make jam and hunker down for the winter? Chop some firewood? Listen to their own thoughts in silence? Honestly, there's no going back to that. There's guilt around letting your kids use technology, but also, sometimes we just need a goddamn break, and it's near impossible to not give in to your kids' incessant pleas for screen time. Sometimes the battle to get them to—for the love of God—try reading a book or play with each other feels totally fruitless. And if we're being honest, we love screen time, too! Sometimes we'll be sitting in the family room together and I'll look up and realize I'm on my phone and my kids are all on their phones, and I really do feel like we're all in a *Black Mirror* episode. It's horrible, scary. But those times when you have the full attention of your kids? Well, it's simply too much pressure. You have no barrier, you're fully available. At least if we have a phone, it's like, okay sorry, Mommy's busy for a second! (Busy online shopping . . .)

## CAT

But of course there are boundaries we need to set up. When my kids start acting like dickbags, that's when I know it's time for screen time to be over. We have to teach kids the correlation between the internet and how the internet makes them feel, not only so they can learn to follow the boundaries we set, but to make boundaries for themselves. We all know social media is addictive—video games are like legal cocaine for kids. And we probably don't have to tell you that overdosing on Instagram can cause self-confidence and inferiority issues. Our kids are being stimulated constantly, and it can have off-screen effects on their mood and mental health. When you keep this in mind, you can be better prepared to see if their behavior is corresponding to the content they're consuming, instead of just thinking your kids are being bad out of nowhere. Working from home a lot of the time, Nat and I have the privilege of being able to watch our kids' moods turn. But for all parents, especially parents who aren't working from home or stay-at-home, one of our main pieces of advice is to get on the social media your kids are on. You don't have to enjoy it, you don't have to do it all the time, and you don't have to be entertained by it (although disliking it will be harder than you think—people on the internet are hilarious). But being a part of these platforms lets you know how their algorithms work and lets you see what kinds of things your kids are consuming. We like to follow a lot of the accounts our kids are following so we know exactly what they're seeing. Incorporating these new technologies into your life may seem like a totally overwhelming thing to do, but ultimately, it'll be worth it to feel more connected to what your kid is seeing every day.

## NAT

For better or worse, these little supercomputers we carry in our pockets are a part of our day and age. After all, you can't just opt out of the time you're living in—otherwise I would've opted out of every fashion choice I ever made pre-2010. And as we know, technology isn't all bad. Cat and I have made our careers and our community using technology. It can be a wonderful platform for connection, for fun, and for broadening horizons. Those same positives apply to our kids' experiences with technology as well. They bond and make friends through video games, they communicate and have social groups through FaceTime or group chats, and they can learn so damn much if they're curious about something you may not have all the answers to. There's a diversity in voices and there's a lot more information about a variety of experiences. It can be a conduit for real-life experiences and knowledge, not just a time sucker. If you hold them back from that, they could miss out on something that could be really great. So try to remember that tech doesn't have to be all doom and gloom—but put the kibosh on anything that seems creepy, and pull out a board game every once in a while (and if you're as competitive as we are, expect tears).

FOUR

# Is Your Husband Your Best Friend?

*Nat*

**Confession:** *"Don't get me wrong, I love my boyfriend. We have SO much fun together and he really is the perfect guy. But he always says to me, "I love you, you're my best friend," and I never know what to say back. Of course I love him, it's the second part that just isn't true lol. I've been avoiding saying it back to him for six years now. Should I break it to him that he's my boyfriend, not my BEST friend?" –Anonymous*

To wind down after a long day, I'll sometimes give my brain a much needed break by watching the delicious reality TV show that is *Love Island*. You know, that show where a bunch of young, dysfunctional, hot people are thrown together on an island and inevitably find true love? It's incredible, and one of the only things I love on this earth. The part that always makes Cat and me die laughing is that without fail, almost every couple on this sexy little island paradise says to each other at some point, with the serious tone of a kid who doesn't want to put their winter coat on, "Gavin/Chelsea/whatever your name is . . . you're, like, my best friend."

Your best friend?! Really, Gavin/Chelsea/whatever your name is? You've known each other what, seven days? A best friend title is something you *earn*, something you *work for*, something you get after taking her to the emergency room at five a.m. in a blizzard because she thinks she drank too much while on antibiotics. It's an award bestowed upon you after you cover for her to your mom acquaintances when she's late to the baseball game because she's getting her butthole waxed. It's something that really cements when you burp each other's babies. A best friend isn't even someone you marry—it's someone you sneak away from your marriage to shoot the shit with. I've always felt this way, and when I hear couples gush about being one another's BFF, I've wondered, what kind of moron would think that a best friend is someone you're in a relationship with?

And then during a crazy-busy time at home, my husband very sweetly plans a date night for us. He books us a table at one of our favorite restaurants in Toronto and orders our favorite dishes. I, for my part, put on a bra that I even washed. Partway through this lovely romantic evening, he takes my hand and looks me in the eyes. I brush my long locks from my face, bat my eyelashes, getting the sense that he's about to say something sweet and romantic: how beautiful I look, how amazing a mother I am, a joke about how he's praying that dressing up plus wine means he might get lucky, etc. Instead, he looks at me and says the words every girl fears: "Nat, you know—you really are my best friend."

Freeze frame. Time stops. My stomach drops. Your best friend? He means this, I know, as a compliment. In the modern world of gender equality and couples therapy and coparenting, I know this moniker is meant to be sweet, an indication of our partnership and progressiveness. Proof of our closeness, our fairy-tale meant-to-be-ness, our total compatibility. But to me, it's like, dude, read the room. I'm trying to seduce you here. I put on a push-up bra and that new influencer lipstick for this. BFF is not the vibe I'm going for. This seems to be a common question in many relationships. Is your partner, someone you've decided to merge your romantic life, your family life, and your financial life with, really a best friend?

When I hear the words "best friend," the first place my mind goes is obviously to Cat. That's why we made grown-up versions of those middle school best friendship necklaces and gave them out on tour—because friendship doesn't get less important as you get older, it actually gets *more* important.

There are just certain things we rely on each other for that fall outside romantic partner territory. First of all, if I'm my husband's best friend, who can he bitch to about me? The best friend has the precarious job of agreeing with your bitching (*He's a total asshole for not unloading the dishwasher and I'm never speaking to him again. I can't believe he was so late to pick up the kids! He got the wrong kind of yogurt?* Dick.) but then knowing when to switch back into we-love-your-husband mode (*He really is looking fit recently! Omg, he got you a couples massage for your anniversary and then didn't even talk during it? Literally the cutest man ever*). Your bestie is always on your side, and knows when to just nod and pour the wine.

There are certain things I wouldn't do with my partner. Like taking a bath. Do I want his giant feet and hairy bod in there with me? What is this, some commercial for a spa weekend? But would Cat and I sit in my Jacuzzi tub in our bathing suits telling each other our darkest secrets? Hell yeah. And where are our husbands in this scenario? Refilling our prosecco.

And I would never, ever lie to Cat. What would be the point

of that? But when my husband asks how much my new gorgeous pair of shoes was, it's just necessary to bend the truth. Would I tell him about the horrible diarrhea I had while at his parents' house? Or my ingrown toenail? Probably not, but I'm definitely texting Cat from the bathroom. Our partners *think* they want to be our best friends, that they want the nitty-gritty of girlhood, but they don't.

There are certain things I'd never do with my best friend, either. Like sex. Sorry, Cat. And on the more practical side, what about financial planning? "Honey, do we think enrolling all the kids in summer camps is going to ruin our savings goals?" That's not a question you ask your best friend.

Your best friend is someone you have bad, nonpractical ideas with. Like, really bad ideas. Naughty, I-can't-believe-we-came-up-with-that bad ideas. Simply speaking, partners say no, and best friends say yes. Getting into trouble together, making fools of ourselves and laughing about it, biting off more than we can chew—these are things a best friend is really for. Nothing says best friendship like bad choices.

The sad thing is, I probably am my husband's best friend. We have this weird tendency in our society—I blame *The Bachelor*—to focus on romantic partnership as the primary relationship in our lives. That our husbands or wives or life partners are our one and only, and should fulfill all roles for us: sexual, romantic, comedic, intellectual stimulation. That we should have the same interests as them, be able to take all the same vacations and go to the same movies as them, cook with them, have all our inside jokes with them. But the reality is, that's a lot of pressure to put on one person!

It's borderline dangerous and should be ILLEGAL to expect one singular person to fulfill all those things. As women, it's natural to have a variety of people, a community of people, in our lives to serve our needs in different ways at different times. Our husbands and our best friends are both deeply important to us—they just occupy different roles.

For women, it's generally expected and encouraged that we have close emotional bonds with one another, and friendships develop out of close emotional bonds. For me and Cat, that bond began when we were both in a difficult place becoming mothers and needed to share that burden with someone else who would really understand it. The emotional closeness we formed by being vulnerable with each other at that difficult time allows us to have lots of crazy adventures together now without any boundaries or awkwardness. We FaceTime while on the toilet, we hold hair back when the other's puking, we share clean underwear on vacation.

It's not that men can't or don't have this, but it's definitely not as common. Men aren't encouraged to talk about their emotions with one another. They don't share every time they have a disagreement with their partner, or deal with a bitchy person, or can't fit into their jeans 'cause they've secretly been eating a doughnut every morning after the kids go to school (that is about NO ONE specific). Men say this bizarre shit about their wives being their best friends because for them, it's true—the person they're most vulnerable and open with in their lives is us. Which is super touching, and something we should always keep in mind. But does it mean that they have to be our besties too? Nah.

Do we have to *tell* them that, though? Up to you—you know

your hubs best, and if it's going to hurt his feelings or you think he won't get it, a white lie can go a long way here.

As for me, back at the dinner table? He looks so sincere telling me I'm his best friend, and the candlelight is so beautiful, and the wine is so good. So I look at him and say, "Sweetie, I love you so much, but we both know who my best friend is, and she's not here right now. She's probably at home texting me about *Love Island*."

# FIVE

# What Happens in Walmart Stays in Walmart

**Confession:** *"I was in the grocery store and my kid was just going crazy. Screaming, crying, and nothing seemed to be able to calm her down. It was so embarrassing, and I started to get looks from other shoppers like, Control your child! So I said, loud enough that they could hear, "If you don't stop, I'm going to tell your mother!" As if I were an aunt or a babysitter. Might have been a bit confusing for my kid, and I feel slightly shitty about it, but sometimes those stares are just too much!" –Anonymous*

S hopping. One word that, as a mom, could mean two completely different things. There are two types of shopping, and they are so different from each other, it's hard to believe they exist in the same space-time continuum. Let's start with the fun one. There's the kind of shopping that you do with your girlfriends on a leisurely Saturday, cappuccinos in hand. Strolling along, plucking pretty bright things from racks, defending each other against snobby salesgirls, encouraging each other to spend over budget because *we deserve it* (and you also want to feel better about having spent so much yourself), stopping for an obligatory post-shop cocktail to congratulate ourselves for . . . something or other.

Now that you have that gorgeous fantasy in your head, let's talk about the other kind of shopping. The real, day-to-day kind of shopping. The kind you're doing not out of desire, but out of duty. A great example of this is a little story that happened to me when my kids were a few years younger than they are now. Flash back to when my youngest daughter was still in diapers.

It's a Thursday of my life. Low on groceries but also in need of that random assortment of items a mom always seems to need (socks, new water bottles, shaving cream, Elmer's glue to feed the ongoing slime obsession my kids have fallen into that I'm too lazy to stop). I'm supposed to be meeting up with Nat later. I tell her I'll just be popping into Walmart for a few minutes with the kids, then dropping them off for playdates and will be over to her house soon. Just a quick errand. Oh, how foolish. It's never that easy, is it?

The automatic doors open and I have two of my three children at my side. Grab a cart, hoist the youngest one in. So far, so good. But the seat isn't comfortable, Mom! No, like really not comfortable! Can I walk? Moments later, he is tired from walking. Already. Then, on the way to the produce section, while I'm trying to convince myself I'll *definitely* use this mega bag of baby arugula before it spoils this time, it will not end up in the compost, I swear, I turn around and my son has flown the coop. Where on earth is he? We're five minutes in and I'm already going to have to put out a missing child report.

My daughter starts squirming and screaming in the cart. If this weren't so embarrassing, I'd frankly be impressed that her small body can produce such a mind-bendingly loud sound. No microphone needed for this kid! If any agents are reading this, she also does an incredible Mariah Carey impression! Now it's time to bring out the big guns. Bargaining. Sweetie, you need to calm down. If you don't calm down, I tell her, you won't be allowed to go to Sara's for a playdate today. But oh shit, that one actually backfires on me—because if she doesn't go to Sara's, then I'm going to have to deal with her for the rest of the day. Rookie mistake. Playdates are God's gift to parents, and skipping one is as much a punishment for you as it is for them. Thankfully, toddlers have short memories.

The screaming goes on, and I can tell I'm really starting to get some looks. Like, real major stink eye. Are-you-even-fit-to-be-with-a-child kind of daggers. These people have no idea the balancing act it takes to haul two full humans with you while you try to compare Walmart's tampon prices with Costco's, wondering when menopause will finally hit.

One last approach left, the mother of all approaches: bribery. Yes, maybe it's not the most becoming look to be able to control your child only by offering them a range of treats, but all's fair in love and war and shopping at Walmart on a Thursday. Okay, what do you want, kid? Pick your poison. Ice cream? Bag of chips? Fuzzy peaches? A $30 DVD we'll never watch? An army of scantily clad L.O.L. dolls?

I'm so embroiled in this negotiation that I almost forget about my son, loose in the giant maze of this department store. That is, until I hear a crash. I frantically look around, hoping he hasn't broken something too expensive or fallen under an on-sale grill. That's when a woman walks over to me. She looks put together in a way I am very much not, probably in her sixties, comfortable but classy shoes, large purse that I bet she never forgets to put her car keys in, seems like she still does hot yoga or something because her body is tight. I think she's going to tell me what a loser of a mother I am that I lost a child and can't even get the one in my sight to just shut the eff up for two minutes until I can grab some goddamn produce and popcorn. As I'm prepping for the lecture, thinking how I can use it as a passionate Insta rant on how judged parents are in public, she smiles at me.

"I hope you don't mind," she says, "I just told your child that he needs to be more well-behaved for his mother while you're shopping. He's cleaning up the cereal boxes he knocked over." I look past her and do indeed see my son stacking Cheerios back on a shelf like some weird little employee. Who is this woman? Is this one of those ghosts-of-Christmas-future moments?

She gives me a little pat on the shoulder, a smile, and a look like, *I get it, I've been there.* My son is sheepishly walking back over to us, may as well have the word "GUILTY" written all over his face. He gives my waist a hug, trying to compensate with his cuteness. This woman has diverted the attention of my daughter enough that she's finally stopped yelling. Before I can say thank you, she's disappeared into the baking aisle like a humble Jedi.

What this interaction proved to me is that motherhood is like being an overworked, unpaid secret agent. We may look like normal people, but we have been to the dark side and back; we've seen and done shit that can't be unseen or undone, and these civilians giving us glares while our kids freak out in the store have no idea what it takes. We got initiated into the club the moment we met our children, looked around, and realized that every single day, this beautiful human's life is relying on *us.* Even when they choose to be unruly, loud, annoying, embarrassing, or all of the above.

Nat's daughter used to throw major temper tantrums, and

in the thick of the storm, people would say to Nat, "You look so calm!" She was always like, "Yes, I keep myself calm, because I'm a trained soldier, I'm an expert, but on the inside, I'm losing my shit."

A few weeks later, I'm shopping at Walmart again. I'm alone for once. Oh, the lovely feeling of solitude! Who knew that shopping at Walmart alone, after that stunt weeks prior, could feel just as luxurious as one of my girls-trip shopping sprees? As I'm taking my time, pondering whether it'd be a total waste of money to get this knockoff-brand lingerie called Shannon's Whisper, I see a mother with three little assholes crawling around her feet, spilling out of her cart, yelling the trademark "MOM MOM MOM WATCH THIS" while she's desperately reaching for some quinoa, dropping her purse, grocery list falling to the floor. She, of course, is getting those judgment eyes from the teenage girl down the aisle and the clearly very single middle-aged guy hoarding chicken fingers in his cart. I feel for this woman. So I walk over, pick up her grocery list and purse from the floor, and say, "Do you want me to watch your cart for a second? And the children attached to it? Don't worry, I'm not, like, a creep."

She pauses for a second, looking me up and down, the evidence of motherhood clear in my messy hair and cart filled with bear claws. She agrees I don't appear to be a creep. "Oh, um, yes, actually, thank you so much," she says. "That's so nice. I just have one thing to grab, I'll be right back. Thank you."

I stand with this woman's three children for a minute as she walks just down the aisle to get the last things on her list and think, Why don't we help each other out like this all the time?

"You should be nicer to your mommy when she's shopping,

'kay?" I tell the kids. They stare at me blankly, but I feel like they get the point.

So I'd like to propose that when we enter a store, we treat it like we mothers, people with other humans as our turbulent accessories, have formed an alliance. The calm aisle browsers, the podcast-listening singles, the hand-holding couples sweetly shopping for organic kale, they have no idea what a task it is to manage your own leaking and screaming carousel of never-ending needs while also going down five wrong aisles in search of paper towels. Give the fellow parents a nod, a smile, an exasperated look of acknowledgment, a finger gun to the head (okay, that last one might be a bit much, but the cool parents think it's funny). We can protect each other against the harsh judgment of those people who have no idea what a task it is to simply get groceries, even if just by letting them know they're not in it alone. If grocery stores were really made for moms, they'd give us a Xanax on our way in and a complimentary bottle of wine on our way out.

SIX

# Never Have I Ever

**Confession:** *"I did some bad stuff as a teenager, like . . . bad. Something involving Jell-O shots and private property destruction comes to mind. And I feel like I'm over-correcting with my kids. Being so strict and worried about them doing bad stuff. I don't want to be not-fun, but I'm so scared of what they might get into."* –Anonymous

The year is 1997. We're in high school. Maybe we're at a party, everyone's a few rounds of beer pong in, the music is starting to lull, energy is dipping. Or maybe it's a girls-only sleepover and we've just run out of pineapple wine coolers and fresh gossip about who on the soccer team Heather hooked up with this year. (Names have been changed and quite frankly we would have gotten them wrong anyway.) There comes a point in the night where someone suggests the classic teenage game Never Have I Ever. The premise is this: you sit in a circle with your friends (or field hockey teammates, secret crushes, sworn rivals, etc.), raise both hands with all ten fingers up in front of yourself, and go around saying "Never have I ever . . . [blank]." The blank should be something scandalous. Never have I ever . . . done a keg stand. Given a blow job. The deeds get more risqué and elaborate as the game goes on. If you *have* done the deed in question, you must put a finger down. Then, if prompted, you have to tell the story that caused you to put your finger down. The first person to have all their fingers down loses in shame (or rather, how we like to think of it, wins for being cool as hell).

It's been a while since either of us have thought of that game. Whether you find it fun or traumatizing, it's undeniably the best way to get dirt about your classmates. Mike lost his virginity to a girl on vacation in *eighth grade*? Sarah was fingered at the movie theater?! Jess stole her entire makeup collection from the drugstore?? (Respect, Jess.) But with our kids fast approaching the age of teendom, our little Never Have I Ever confessions are more present in our minds lately.

## CAT

One day I'm walking downtown to meet Nat, and this group of kids is in front of me. I mean, it isn't my fault that this is a peak eavesdropping opportunity—they're going the same direction as I am, and I forgot my AirPods! What am I supposed to do, plug my ears? These kids are around the same age as Nat's daughter, at this point about twelve or thirteen. Total preteens—braces and all. But their conversation? Shockingly teenage. They're talking about how they're planning on getting drunk and don't want their parents to know. Ironing out all those logistical details that come with underage debauchery: *Whose older sister is buying us alcohol? Whose basement are we going to? When are your parents coming home from their trip?* I was shocked! Twelve years old, and already sneaking around drinking alcohol? I had to tell Nat.

I get to the coffee shop and fill her in. She laughs in my face.

"Are you kidding me? Cat, come on. Don't you remember us at that age?"

I think back. Who, me? I was an angel!

Nat takes a sip of her coffee. "Did I ever tell you about the time I did 'shrooms while babysitting?"

I shake my head.

"Oh my God, I can't believe I haven't, that's a classic story. So I used to babysit for the neighbors when I was like, fourteen, with a friend of mine. One day we were set to babysit and we were like, how can we make this more fun? We decided it would be awesome to take 'shrooms. Neither of us had done it before, being fourteen, and I honestly have no idea how we even got them. But after the kids were sleeping, we ate them. In retrospect, we were idiots. 'Shrooms last so long, way longer than the parents were going to be gone for. So we started tripping, and remember that it's supposed to feel really good to be outside when you're on 'shrooms. Being one with nature, etc. We're having a great time like, *feeling the grass* and stuff, definitely not a boring night, when I have to pee. I walk up to the house to go inside and realize . . . we've locked ourselves out. Which means we've locked ourselves out, and we've locked the little kids we're babysitting *in*! We had to call the parents and get them to come home from dinner to unlock the door. At least they didn't suspect we were absolutely tripping out on 'shrooms."

And just like that, we're dunked back into our wild days. Over our lattes, we start to remember a stream of sneaking around, secret bags of illicit substances, cheap mall lingerie hidden from our parents.

"Oh God!" I say to Nat, covering my face with my hands as the memories flood in. "I just remembered how at school dances, me and my friends used to chug bottles of wine in the bathroom and hide them in the tampon dispensers. At school!"

"You think that's bad?" Nat says. "I remember in grade eleven, we had a school trip to NYC, and one of the girls on the trip was a total raver. Days before the trip, she tells a group of us that she can get cocaine to bring. *Across the border?* Yep, no problem. She literally put cocaine in her tampon box to cross the border. Then before we went to the Empire State Building with our teachers, we did cocaine! That's the one thing about being a teenage girl—you can really use your period to get out of a lot. We call that being resourceful."

We cackle. But then Nat turns to me. She says she can't believe the girls I saw were her daughter's age.

"Is she really getting to that point already? We were doing crazy stuff at what, fifteen? That's not far off for her."

## NAT

I walk home thinking about how to talk to my daughter about what Cat told me. The tweens her age, already sneaking around with alcohol. At thirteen! But judging by how Cat and I behaved, it won't be long before much worse gets introduced to the mix. We were doing hard drugs in high school! Parenting at that time was a lot more hands-off. In our glory days, parents turned a blind eye, or they didn't really want to deal with it, or they just had absolutely no clue. Before cell phones, you never knew where your kids were, and that was normal! But now? I basically track my kids like I'm the NSA.

I get home and my daughter's in her room. I go upstairs and sit down on her bed with her.

"Sweetie," I say, "I just want to talk to you about something. Cat was telling me today that she walked behind these kids your age, maybe even who go to your school, who were talking about getting drunk with their friends and hiding it from their parents. I just want to bring this up to you so we can keep an open conversation going between us. If you ever have friends talking like this, you can talk to me about it."

I knew it would be an awkward conversation, but it's a necessary one. Instead of being surprised when things like this come up with friends, I want her to be prepared. *You and your friends are going to get your periods. Your friends are going to smoke drugs.* That kind of thing. But I didn't anticipate how much my daughter would be caught off guard by this one. She had a physical rejection to the idea that kids her age would be doing that kind of thing. She's sure that Cat must have got it wrong, that they couldn't be her age— she's way too young for that kind of thing. She's not a goody-goody, but this was maybe the first time that the reality that she's really growing up sets in. The idea that kids would start doing things that parents do, like drink, is really uncomfortable for her. It's a totally fair reaction, but one I didn't expect.

"I just don't want to be a part of all that right now," she tells me.

Fair enough! But at least now she knows, and she knows I know, so she can talk to me about it.

I see Cat later and we debrief.

"So it turns out," I say, after explaining the conversation with my daughter, "that our kids might be way more tame than we were."

She laughs.

"That's so classic for us. We're like, grilling our kids for information, and they're just being normal kids having a good time playing with dolls and shit. They'll have their friends over and we're going to burst in on them being like, 'YOU'RE HIGH! What's in your drink!' Meanwhile, it'll literally just be Snapple. The kids will be like, 'Mom, my friends are coming over, can you just tone it down? We're truly only watching a movie.'"

Then Cat tells me she's been thinking more about those upcoming teenage years, and sorting through the indiscretions she could live with and the ones she couldn't.

"So there's going to be a point where they have sex. I'm not naive enough to think that's never going to happen. But if they do it, they gotta WRAP IT UP. Don't you dare get pregnant or get someone else pregnant—that is a long-term decision."

"Yeah, that one's a given," I say. "No one's making me a grandma before I'm at least like, sixty. And what about drugs?"

"I'd feel like a hypocrite, expecting them to never experiment when Lord knows I did," Cat muses, "but I was an idiot to experiment as a teen—it's so easy for things to go wrong, and kids are dumbasses. I'd hope the absolute max hardest drug they ever try in their life is cocaine, and only as an adult once their brains are fully cooked. And even then, only if they *really* want to, and only with a trusted, cocaine-experienced friend." She stops. "But then again, do I want them to have cocaine-experienced friends?"

I laugh. "Whatever, we'll cross that bridge when we come to it."

Cat continues, "One piece of advice that may sound weird but is actually so important: I really wouldn't want them to have just one boyfriend or girlfriend their whole lives. Don't fall in love and stay with that person all the way through forever. The teenagers who are still dating the person they started fake-dating in grade five and like, never talk to anyone else? Gross!" She makes a face. "The people who are married to their grade-nine sweetheart and change their life around them? No thank you! Don't miss out on traveling because they can't come with you, don't stay home from that incredible party because they have to get up early for work the next day. Live your life! Don't give up at nineteen!"

"Amen to that!" I say, hands in the air. "Young love is cute, but it shouldn't be everything."

"And finally," Cat says, "never, ever, ever drink and drive. This goes for weed and driving, too. Just do not do it. It's dumb and irresponsible and awful. Oh, and no hitchhiking either."

Cat has now laid out the guidelines we'll use to claw our way through our kids' teenage years, and I already feel better just having talked about where we stand. "You know," I say to her, "when I was growing up, my mom definitely gave me the impression that if you do anything *bad*, naughty, rebellious, you won't turn out to be a successful person. A lot of parents think like that—that if you get into trouble as a teen, you'll be living at home forever, or you'll be blocked from entering civilized society. That you're guaranteed to have all sorts of issues. You and I are from split families. Every single one of our siblings and stepsiblings did a lot of naughty things, but we all turned out okay! There must be something to teaching your kids core values that they can hold on to, and guidelines they can follow as they go through making tricky, even bad, decisions."

Cat agrees. "And you know," she says, "so much of teen and tween behavior is shameful only because *no one talks about it*. If kids don't know where the boundaries are, they think we're going to freak out and lock them away for every little thing they do, and they'll never tell us the truth about what's going on or come to us for help." She goes on. "And parents get caught up in something similar—they think that no one else's kid is struggling in school, or going through challenges with their mental health, or bucking the system in some way. FYI, every child is bucking the system! Your kids are just finding themselves, even if they're making you crazy by acting out in order to get there. You're not a fuckup as a parent if your kid's room stinks of weed. Those rules I came up with are great, but I also want my kids to know that if you fail, it doesn't mean *you're* a failure. It just means you went down a dead end. You need to turn around and find another route. Everything you and I have done led us to being the people we are now. I'm not pushing or encouraging drugs and alcohol, I'm just saying that the kids who use them are not inherently bad kids. They just need to be cared for and kept on track."

"You're totally right," I say to Cat. "People look down their street and think no one else has a kid doing the things their kid is doing. But the truth is, it's magical when people share their realities with each other and we realize we're not in it alone."

Though Cat and I have lost (or won, in our books) every game of Never Have I Ever we've been part of, we turned out pretty fantastic. Look at us now: other people even buy books of semi-helpful, mainly funny advice from us! If that's not a success story, I don't know what is. So if you had experiences that would make you lose a game of Never Have I Ever, don't forget to let your kids have some, too. Who knows—maybe one day you can compare notes and play the game together.

# SEVEN

# Running the Show

**Confession:** *"I am always parenting while at work. AL-WAYS! Calls from the school, kids forgetting backpacks, appointment scheduling, mentally prepping what the fuck we're going to eat . . . everything. Once my hubby was out of town so I had to work from home, and I was literally holding a bowl for my toddler to vomit into while running a conference call. Not to mention the times I feel like I'm parenting my twentysomething employees." –Anonymous*

*an she have it all?* When our business was ramping up to the next level, Cat and I put that age-old question to the test. Can we juggle the 24/7 unpaid job of being a mother with our moneymaking, fun-having business? We were ready to try. Our kids are a little older, and they have grandparents, dads, and babysitters to help carry the load, and we were presented with too exciting an opportunity to pass up. We decided we could put being moms on hold for a week or two at a time while we went on tour to *talk* about being moms with all the parents and caretakers we've fallen in love with online. Armed with our giant water bottles, Advil, and neck pillows, and having left long instructional lists for our husbands, we were ready for our life on the road. City to city, wild night to wild night, we were excited and feeling good. We were basically about to be Madonna, if Madonna lived in activewear. Little did we know, our roles as moms wouldn't so much pause as double.

A large tour bus housed our team and was our home base for these weeklong trips, during which we'd stop in a handful of cities for a day each to do our live show. One flight, taxi ride, and team meeting later, we were sitting on the bus, our shades on and our headphones in. Time to take out our phones and zone the hell out.

A blissful half hour later, I was deep inside the world of _TikTok_ when my phone started vibrating like crazy.

"Hey Mom," my son says, "we're waiting for the lunches but none have come yet and lunch is almost over."

Oh no no no. I had totally forgotten that in a last-minute rush out the door, realizing we had no lunches prepared for while I was away, I told my kids I'd Uber them lunch to school. Every day. Seemed like a good idea at the time. But I'd completely forgotten.

So much for my downtime. Most of motherhood is just assumed, because you're too busy to think or talk about it, so you just do it. How did we end up with this job? We're not inventory managers or private chefs any more than our husbands are. And yet it's all part of the "mom" job—that's what no one tells you.

I opened the UberEats app and paid $20 extra for "DELIVERY ASAP," and added in the notes "plz my kids will starve" for extra speediness, thousands of miles away, while on a bus with shitty Wi-Fi. This would not be the last time on this trip that we were in a different country than our families but still meal planning and getting food dropped at their door.

And it wasn't just at home that we were managing food consumption. We learned fast that the cardinal sin of the bus was doing a number two in the only bathroom and sticking everyone in a shit-smelling moving vehicle. But if you really had to go and didn't want to be a dick, you had to do the walk of shame up the middle aisle to the driver, pretending you were in desperate need of McNuggets. The poor guy would cross four lanes of traffic to pull into a McDonald's parking lot, and everyone would wait for you while you placed almost a full roll of toilet paper on the disgusting toilet seat before finally sitting down.

Cat and I quickly realized that since we were sleeping on this bus, if we ate a big dinner late at night, we might have an emergency situation on our hands. So we did something only moms know how to do: we came up with a daily routine that was dictated by bowel movements. Without really explaining it to our team, Cat and I took charge of the dining schedule. We didn't even think of this as a weird thing to do. We didn't even consider that it *actually wasn't our responsibility* to monitor everyone's comfort and convenience at all times. We would roll into a new town about midday and stop for lunch before we started prepping for the evening show. Cat and I would sit in the middle of the table and order for everyone. "One of everything," that was our motto. We'd eat as much as we possibly could for lunch, and make it our main meal of the day. It was like we were hearkening back to farm times, when dinner was in the middle of the day to give you the sustenance to move on and keep working. Which was true, but also, in our case, it was to give you the relief of knowing you wouldn't have to shit in front of your entire professional peer group. It became so much the norm that when a new team member joined us and was waffling about what to order, *this close* to getting a lame salad, one of the veteran team members whispered to them, "Don't even bother thinking about it. We're eating our biggest meal now, and Cat and Nat get us one of everything." For some reason (the reason being, uh, the expectations of motherhood), we took on the role of making sure everyone was on track, on schedule, fed and digested properly.

The next day, we're on the road again when I get a call.

My oldest daughter is calling me, and immediately I'm like, Oh God, oh no, she got her period, didn't she? Before I left, I had prayed she wouldn't get her period while I was gone, calling on any goddess of the Aunt Flow variety to wait until I could be there to help her not freak out about blood coming out of her vagina, but here it is, my penalty for leaving my kids, even if just for a week. I answer the phone and she sounds teary. This is it.

Instead she unloads a complicated web of friendship drama so intense, it sounds like an episode of *Riverdale* (which I only watched two seasons of, because I'm an ADULT). Tweens sure know how to raise the stakes! I get her to slow down and walk me through everything that's happened. I can tell that one of these girls is insecure and is taking it out on the people around her in order to feel better about herself. Being mean in order to gain confidence—oldest trick in the book. We talk about it for a while, even thinking of some steps to take and a conversation they can have to work it out. Then the bus pulls up to our venue and I kiss her goodbye through the phone. A successful working-mom moment, if I do say so myself.

That night after the show, I'm feeling so good about both work and mom life, realizing we CAN have it all, when I hear something coming from the bunk bed next to mine on the bus. At first I wonder if Cat is having that sex dream again where all the New Kids On The Block show up at her house, but then I look over to see . . . two of our teammates making out. I silently scream, text Cat, who, I can tell by the thump I get from her bottom bunk, is also silently screaming.

The next day, we're flying home to see our kids, one of the many times we took red-eye flights to get back and mom. A few weeks later, when everyone returns to the tour bus for our next leg, something feels off. We sense it in the air almost immediately. The two smoochers—one older team member of ours and one newer—are clearly not talking. No one else on the team seems to notice this but us. Mom radar.

Cat and I decide to pull the team member we've known longer aside and ask them what's up. We say in our gentle mom-voices that we noticed there might be some tension between them and the other person, and ask if we can do anything to help. Now, perhaps it's the spirit of the tour we're on, the confessional nature of our shows, and our tendency to tell everyone around us everything we're thinking all the time, but our teammate tells us everything. Suddenly it's like we're the tour-bus Dr. Phil, easing the communication, proposing different tactics, trying to keep everyone calm. I even started a rousing round of "Wheels on the Bus."

Finally, we realize the inevitable. We could not escape being mothers just by being away from our kids, at work, with grown adults. We can't turn it off because it's not a job title: it's part of who we are now. Being a mother never leaves you, once you are one. No matter where you are or what you're doing, it's part of your DNA. Whatever the day may hold, we bring our mothering skills to the table in one way or another. During our tour, we were mothers in two ways: professionally and personally. Deciding what our teammates ate and when they ate it, and managing conflict. You may have many other incredible attributes to offer, but you've gained a huge (and underappreciated) skill set from those hard-learned lessons of being a mom. You know how to keep things running smoothly, how to keep everyone's basic needs met, how to juggle emotional turmoil, how to get the show on the road. We see it in so many of the moms we meet, some who scrub into surgery after staying up all night to get Disney on Ice tickets, some who leap back into work three months postpartum, some who run the business of their homes and families better than Fortune 500 CEOs ever could. The old saying works just as well for business as it does for motherhood: Ladies and gentlemen, the show must go on.

# EIGHT

# Get Ready with Us

**Confession:** *"I swear to God, if I open up YouTube and see another fucking fresh-faced twenty-four-year-old model going through her eighty-seven-step morning skincare routine, I'm going to throw up. What's with these elaborate, calming morning routines? You're telling me they do yoga and make a smoothie every single morning??? They do an eye mask? Moisturize? How the fuck do they know what products to buy and why do they have a hundred tiny pastel bottles on their marble vanities? Magazines, Instagram . . . everywhere, there are these gorgeous girls talking about how they get ready, and I'm like, when was the last time I had ANY routine, let alone a MAKEUP ROUTINE?! I'm lucky if I remember to shit. Where the hell are the REAL get-ready routines?"* –Anonymous

Hi guys, and welcome to our channel! Today we're going to take you through Cat and Nat's Signature Get Ready with Us Routines. Whether it's a calming yet invigorating start to your morning or a fun and cheeky beginning to your night out, we're here to take you through how we get ready, and give you some fun tips along the way!

## CAT'S DAILY MORNING RITUAL

Hi guys! A lot of you have been asking, "How do you do it? What's your secret to looking THAT good and being THAT emotionally stable?" Well, wonder no further, I've laid out my daily morning rituals here for you.

I like to start off with a terrible night's sleep. This could be caused by one of my kids having a bad dream, or just the swirling inferno of thought spirals in my mind. I like to sometimes throw in waking up in a sheer panic at four a.m. realizing the tooth fairy forgot to do her job, or maybe wondering if I ever changed the laundry from the washer to the dryer. Fun things like that. You can sub in whatever variation you want, but MAKE SURE you are awakened with heart-pounding anxiety at least once a night for the full Cat-experience! And once I've tossed and turned and built up a nice layer of cold, clammy sweat, I like to sink into a deep sleep at approximately six thirty a.m.

Then, just on time, my alarm jolts me awake at six forty-five a.m. Or even better, to change it up (variety is the spice of life, am I right!), some mornings one of my kids will tap at my shoulder so hard that I wake up with a nice rush of adrenaline! How did they get so strong! It feels like they're trying to dig through ice! I then roll over and wonder how long they've been gawking at me. Usually they're breathing heavily and staring eerily from the corner, already desperately needing something from me even though they've only been awake for a minute and thirty seconds. Or sometimes they even hide in the curtains until I'm awake and then jump out to scare me. So what I'm saying is, I like to start my mornings with pain, fear, and/or immediately being asked to do something before I even realize I'm conscious. The beautiful thing about this is you don't even need to set an alarm, ladies!

At this point, my eyes are typically glued shut from how much sugar I ate last night, so I rub them and realize how dehydrated I am. I think about drinking a glass of water but in about five seconds, forget to get one. I don't have time to shower, of course, so I put my hair up using whatever's on my nightstand, usually a JoJo Siwa scrunchie or a plain elastic band. My favorite style is this really chic look called a messy bun. So versatile! Who knew your hair could go in that many directions?

Then I don't even think about opening my closet. I would much prefer to not get dressed at all, but apparently that's legally required when I drop my kids off at school, so I look for the path of least resistance. I search for the most comfortable, widest, most elastic-y panties I can find. Preferably beige, with various old stains. I believe they're clean. I then look past the many pretty bras I've purchased over the past decade to get my trusty loose, comfortable bra from a brand I don't think exists anymore that I wear every day and don't wash. Next, pants. Ah yes, my leggings that are on the ground, PERFECT. The mental energy it would take me to select a new pair of pants from my closet is too much to ask. Yes, I may have worn these yesterday, and yes, they might have food on them. But I could just as easily get egg yolk on them this morning while making breakfast, so if I leave with food on them, no one will know it was from yesterday and not this morning. Right? See, I love to do a little philosophical thinking in the morning as well.

I *almost* think about putting on real clothes, but then I remind myself that I might—perhaps, in some multiverse—work out today. So in that case, okay, leggings it is. I guess what I'm saying is, I basically have one of those minimalist capsule wardrobes where each pair of leggings works with each baggy top (if you ignore my closet filled with real-people clothes that I wear on special occasions, like holiday parties or when I see my hot dentist).

Next, I like to do some intention setting. You know, like really clearing your mind and focusing on the things you want most, willing them into existence. I recommend saying those things as mantras to yourself. Stuff like, "I am going to be calm today," "I'm not going to yell at the kids today," "I'm going to be organized today, I am going to get ahead of everything," "I am going to sit down with a tea and read a chapter of a book today," "I'm going to finish my cup of coffee instead of leaving it half-drunk on the bathroom counter only to find it cold and stained with rings when I'm about to collapse into bed, mocking the morning's attempts at Zen." Then I look in the mirror and laugh. We both know that's not true! It's good to start the day with a little humor.

Now it's time for the pièce de résistance: my skincare routine. I rub my eyes with water, brush my teeth, and smear what might be Bath & Body Works Vanilla Bean Noel body cream on my face. Never mind that it's April; I find that it really adds some luxury to your day to use discontinued seasonal scents. You can't just find this stuff in stores!

Now comes the part of my morning ritual that is a little harder to outline. Like the beautiful waves of a tsunami, from seven to eight fifteen a.m., you can never tell what will come crashing over you. A sample of this part of the routine: The kitchen's suddenly a total disaster and I can't find the cereal my daughter likes. Someone's crying because they're anxious about what's happening at school today. There's a full-on brawl between three kids before they've even put their clothes on. I'm sweating already (see, workout clothes pay off), and suddenly someone's yelling that they forgot to print something they absolutely *need* today. And of course, during the height of this, my husband is calling me twice to ask the most stressful, not-time-sensitive things. Like, did we sign our son up for hockey camp? As I get this delightful call, I open my kids' backpacks to put in their lunch and find one or more of these things:

A) A rotten plum that's covered in blue mold.

B) A letter from the school from a week ago that says someone in the class has lice so make sure to check your kids for lice. Great, now my whole family might have lice.

C) A notice that there's a bake sale TODAY and, oh yeah, they forgot to tell me. Well, looks like my craving for boxed grocery store cookies is paying off after all. Throw those babies in a Tupperware and call it a day. It's all the same ingredients as homemade anyways, you know?

Before getting the kids off to their various destinations (relatively on time, most major tantrums resolved, teeth possibly brushed), it's time for my makeup routine! It's what I like to call a two-step process, and it can only be done sitting in the driveway of my house or the school parking lot—location is crucial. Step 1: Throw a bunch of shit onto my hands, rub it on my face, hope for the best. Step 2: Look at myself in the car mirror and say, okay, that was not a good job, and try to fix it by desperately running my fingers over my face some more. Here's a fun trick that'll get you some extra looks: I've been known to put mascara and eyeliner on one side of my face and not the other. Whether it's Nat, the barista at Starbucks, or our Instagram followers calling me out on it, it's nice to know people are paying attention to me!

Next we have the school drop-off. This part is fun because it can absolutely ruin the rest of your day in the blink of an eye. The land mines can come from anywhere: a teacher whispering, "We need to talk later." Your tween's meltdown about forgetting their friend's birthday present—which of course is my problem to solve. Obviously I will save their ass. This is when it's helpful to go back to my morning mantras—I will remain calm. I will not inform my kids that they just ruined my day.

And just as I'm driving away, having saved the day three times over, I get a call from the school office. My son forgot his indoor shoes. Tough luck, kid. I've got to start work! Plus, I just bought you new outdoor shoes, they're nice, show them off! Turn those into your indoor shoes and go outside barefoot. Start a trend! Be inventive!

Then, as I drive to get the overpriced coffee I clearly deserve, I don't even bother to change the trash music my kids were playing in the car. It's not even nine a.m. Good-motherfucking-morning, ladies.

## NAT'S GIRLS-NIGHT-OUT EVENING ROUTINE

Ah, another Saturday night. We all know that when the weekend rolls around, it's time for mom to get her groove on. Kids, those little angels, are tucked away in bed, quietly reading a book as they drift off to sleep, so that Saturday can be all about *me*. Every weekend my girlfriends and I get together *Sex and the City*–style for a big night out. We wear heels and order cosmopolitans and discuss our amazing sexy adventures . . .

Okay, back to reality. As a mom, nights out are few and far between. And from the response we get when we do our live shows, sounds like that's the situation for most moms. I'm lucky to live in the same city as many of my girlfriends, but you'd think we lived in different countries for how often we get together for a night on the town. A night out with your girlfriends is a special, spiritual, magical experience as a mom. Meaning: It's fucking direly needed sometimes. It's an *event*. It's basically more important than prom or your wedding day. And an event of this magnitude requires a look to match. Let me walk you through my girls-night-out evening routine.

A night out is planned and locked down for weeks ahead of time. GNO (girls night out) is like a tiny lighthouse, a beacon I'm staring at while I thrash around in the rocky seas of packing lunches and unloading the dishwasher. Partners are shackled into solo kid duty, we've picked the bar my twenty-year-old babysitter said is "lit," and I'm even considering shaving my legs. Then, finally, the day arrives. I'm like, okay, I just have to get through one more day and then I'm GOING OUT! By eight a.m., I text the group chat that I've named "GIRLS NIGHT OUT" like "ohmygod I'm so excited are you so excited!" and exchange approximately ten thousand dancing girl emojis to get hyped ahead of time.

At about four p.m., I suddenly feel so tired. I wonder, is someone in my family sick? Is there a fever going around? Because honestly, I'm feeling like going out is going to take a lot of effort. This is the second-guessing-the-entire-event part of the routine. It's the part where I realize I'm going to have to put on actual clothes and go see the world. I haven't seen the world in so long! Do I even look normal? This feels incredibly overwhelming. It's also the part in the routine where I realize I don't know what's cool to wear anymore. It's not like I have time to tear apart my closet or scroll through Instagram for ideas, only to feel even worse about myself. I get the urge to buy something new . . . but there's no time. Focus. I look at my kid and he seems a little unhappy. I convince myself he must be sick. I'm going to get them all sick! I'm actually crafting the long apologetic text to my girlfriends trying to let them down easy when they start texting, "What time are we meeting?" and I realize I can't let them down. This will be good for me.

Once the denial section is finished, we move on to Confronting the Partner. My husband comes home and of course has forgotten that I'm going out, though I told him a thousand times, wrote it on a note next to his bed, texted him, and sent an animated e-card to his work email inviting him to a night of taking care of our kids.

When he gets home, he's like, "Why are you all in a tizzy?" And I'm like, "'CAUSE I'M GOING OUT!" And then he chooses this moment as the right time to debrief me on his entire life, what's going on with his coworkers, how he wants to incorporate a new workout his friend told him about into his week. At this point I put my hand on his shoulders and say, "No, honey. This is the time when I need to get ready." And the response is never "You go girl, have the time of your life! You deserve this." No. It's more of a be-grudging acceptance of the reality that I'm leaving him helpless at the mercy of our children for the night.

This is when I feel all sorts of heaviness and guilt and I can't tell if I'm making it up in my head or if my family is actually pissed I'm going out. He doesn't say it, but in my head my husband is asking me a thousand questions. What time are you going to be home? How much are you going to drink? Are you going to be drunk when you get home? I ignore the imaginary questions, because it's time for the next part: makeup!

I always make sure to go upstairs with a glass of wine to block out the guilt (tip: the more wine you drink, the better you look!). At this point, I take a few sips, look at myself in the mirror, and say, Okay, where are we at? Is there a chance we can make this work?

I go to the bathroom. I take out the makeup bag. I take out every powder, tint, face thing I can find. Obviously if I'm going out I need extra coverage. To start my routine I dab things on my face and try to Frankenstein my way into looking like Em Ratajkowski.

I put on some blush and sparkle to up the ante. And finally, the eyeliner. On Instagram anyone who is going out has black eyeliner on, and somehow they're able to take the eyeliner all the way from the inner eye and swoosh it to the outer eye with that little wing, no fuckups, and it looks seamless. I'm a little older now, though I know you wouldn't have guessed, so I get these little skids doing the eye lines because the brush pulls the eyelids and then . . . disaster. Let me find a Q-tip. You seriously think I could find a Q-tip in this house? I pull up a tutorial of how to do eyeliner by a sixteen-year-old on YouTube who looks better than I did on my wedding day (okay, I know this is supposed to be a tutorial from me to you, but think of this more as a pooling of resources).

Next up: a ton of mascara, gloss, lip color. By this point I'm done with my glass of wine and call for my son to grab the bottle. I need a refill, this whole situation is taking way too long. The important thing here for the authentic Nat-experience is to make sure you're covered in sweat by this point. But I can't lie, I look good.

It's clothing time! I walk to the closet to check out what gorgeous threads I'm going to don tonight. There I'll find random pieces left behind from the four hundred times I've cleaned out my closet in the past year (thanks, Marie Kondo). I try the first thing on, can't zip it up. Okay, next one: cute top, too tight on my arms. The next one: amazing dress Cat bought me . . . then I realize it has a rip in it. I love this part of the routine, where I not only get to feel bad about my body, but also wonder where all my cute clothes have gone and whether I even own a single thing worth wearing!

The ugly step tracker I wear as an accessory at this point is going crazy from the workout I'm getting just trying on clothes, so I go lie down on my bed and take deep breaths. Mantra time! I exercise some self-talk: "This isn't a big deal, you're just going to have fun, this isn't a test of, like, your womanhood. No one is judging you. You're going out with your girlfriends, it's going to be great." I've almost achieved calm when my kids run in screaming, "MOM WHAT ARE YOU DOING WHAT ARE YOU WEARING WHERE ARE YOU GOING?" I send them out on a quest to find where the hell their brother is with that wine refill.

Okay, you know what? At this point in the evening, you pull out your secret weapon: Spanx leather pants. They're still leggings, technically, but they're *fancy* leggings. They also keep all the loose bits all nice and tucked in. They are the greatest invention ever made, and if they'd like to sponsor me, I'm very available. I whip on those bad boys and know they'll never let me down. They might not breathe at all, I might sweat like a motherfucker, but at least I look like I'm actually wearing leather pants. I gave it a good ol' college try with the jeans, but at this point they're a foreign object to me.

And let's be honest, everyone's just thinking about themselves and how they look at the bar anyways. Although I might fantasize about how men are going to fall over themselves to chat me up, I'm not cruising, I'm married! Which reminds me, while I have my evening routine going on, I know in the back of my mind that my husband is watching me like a hawk. This is called married foreplay. I'm dressing up, going out for cocktails, and he's thinking,

Okay, my chances are really good tonight. At this point, you might want to remind your partner that these boobies are not for you tonight! These are for my girlfriends! We dress up for each other, and for ourselves. And for all the young people who are going to be at the very lit (but hopefully not *well*-lit) bar to prove I have my shit together. Kind of. You could tell your partner this, or you could just let them have this one.

Time for the last part: hair. I try to do that thing again with the flat iron where you use it to make a wave, thinking maybe this is the time I'll be able to figure it out. Nope. In theory I understand what to do, but something between my brain, my hand, the tool, and my hair just doesn't connect. You know what, straight hair will look better with this outfit anyways.

The next part of the routine is the pre-departure. Finishing the wine and putting my shoes on in the front hall. Sweating, beyond uncomfortable. Are these shoes cool anymore? All the kids are running around saying, "What are you doing, Mom?" The house is getting cozier by the minute. Do I really want to do this? While I'm honestly pondering, the youngest kid comes out of his room, though I've already put him to bed, and says, "Why do you look like that?" Oh God, even a bad review from my kid. "I'm just playing dress up!" I tell him. "Go back to bed!" The older kids also have a lot of questions: "Is anyone going to get drunk tonight? Are you going to get drunk tonight? Are you drunk now?" More grilling: "Which of your friends are you going with? Is that the one that smokes? Does she still smoke, Mom? Are you going to smoke? Does anybody vape?" God, what am I, a teenager?!

If only to get out of these questions, I call my Uber. Inside the Uber, I immediately feel bad that I've left them all behind, and I'm already worrying about being hungover tomorrow. And I haven't even gotten to the restaurant yet.

Oh shit, did I put on deodorant?

# NINE

# Keeping Up with the Joneses

*Nat*

**Confession:** *"My family lives comfortably, but we're by no means mega-rich. My kids are often innocently asking me why they don't have certain things—the newest toys, the newest clothes, fancy vacations, fancy cars—that some of their friends have. I don't know how to explain to them that we just can't afford that kind of lifestyle without freaking them out. I don't want them to think they're any less than their classmates who have loaded parents. I don't know how to talk to them about money without making them worried, but I also don't want to make them feel bad about not having the newest stuff." –Anonymous*

It's a regular Thursday, and I'm picking up my son from school after a meeting with Cat downtown. It's always on one of those quiet days that your kid asks you a question to which the answer is so complicated, so nuanced, you wish you could just answer "because that's just the way it is." But when you become a parent, you opt in to explaining the trickiest aspects of life to another human in a way that doesn't either blind him to reality or damage him irrevocably. My son gets in the car, and while we're driving away from his public school, he asks one of those questions.

"Mom, do kids who go to private school get better jobs than kids who go to public school?"

"Oh gosh, sweetie," I say. "Not necessarily."

"So why would anyone pay all that money to go to private school if they can get just as good jobs going to school for free?"

Now *this* is a hard one to answer. At first, I give him an easy response.

"Well, some kids need extra help, or they need a smaller class size so they can do better in school. You work very well independently, so you don't need that."

I look over at him and can tell he's sensing I'm not giving him the full story. A lot of kids with no academic issues at all go to private school. The real answer? It's because their parents have a lot of money! It's about class, prestige, status. But how do you explain wealth and money to your sweet kid?

Finances are one of those complicated things that even us adults don't totally understand, and that's why it's so hard to explain to our kids. Some people have a lot of money, and some people don't, and then your kids ask why that is, or if the people with more money deserve it more than the people with less. So you say, "No, of course not!" But then they ask why the people with less money don't have the same amount if they deserve it just as much . . . and here we are, trying to delve into the mechanics and morals of economics, privilege, and capitalism—when to be honest, I still don't understand why we can't just print more cash. Trying to convey these complicated topics to children (and eventually to a twentysomething with their first credit card—no, honey, it's not *free* money) is one of the hardest things about being a parent.

Later that day, I'm giving the download on this conversation to my husband. We have our oldest kids in private school, and the younger ones in public school. There are a lot of factors to consider when deciding where to send your kids to school, especially in the big city we live in, where private school comes at a hefty price. When people hear how much private school is in Toronto, they're like, "Are you fucking kidding me? University is cheaper than this!" And at least at university you don't get in trouble for rolling up your uniform skirt!

But as a first-time mom, you're so often totally freaked out about everything, and it's natural to want to give your kid as much as you possibly can. And so, if you can swing it, private school might be part of that conversation. Do you know how many parents think their kid isn't going to be okay in public kindergarten after preschool? Because their child is "just different"? Public school can seem scary—one person, one teacher, looking after thirty children. As a first-time parent, when you can barely take care of one kid yourself, this seems daunting. And it is. But kids are resilient and teachers are angels. If they're in public school, will everyone's tears and noses be wiped? Nope! But as a parent you learn to sometimes be less precious about your kids. And when the alternative is totally financially unfeasible? Well, guess what, they'll be okay in public school.

As I'm talking about this to my husband, he makes a comment about "keeping up with the Joneses." My son walks into the kitchen and overhears this, and asks us what it means.

"You know how when one of your friends has a new toy or video game, you feel like you should also have the same toy or video game?" I tell him. "Or how the family down the street got a black lab dog, and then the other family we know also got a black lab dog? It's the idea that once one family has something, the other families that are in the same social circle feel like they need to have it too, even if they don't really *need* it. Or they can't afford it. Suddenly everyone feels like they need to have a yearly trip to Disney World, or a TV in every room, or an inherited ski chalet in Switzerland where their kids are simultaneously learning French and training for the Olympics."

My husband says that the phrase "keeping up with the Joneses" is such a forever term because people are always comparing themselves to other people they know. We don't mention to my son about how so many people are majorly in debt from just trying to keep everyone happy, healthy, and socially up to snuff—and they'd never let on.

"Yeah, but why can't we all just have all that stuff?" my son asks.

"Well, hon, some parents bring in more money every year than other parents, and so they can afford things that other people can't. You know how there's that family that drives a Ferrari at your brother's school, and we don't? That's not because your dad wouldn't love a Ferrari."

It's a tricky thing to explain. When my older son showed up to private school, his eyes were opened to a whole other way of living. Parents dropping their kids off in Lambos like it was no big deal. This kind of thing can make kids insecure, especially when they don't understand why they don't have something.

He still doesn't seem to be getting how this all fits together. I decide to tell him a story.

"When I was younger," I tell him, "our family moved into a

new house. We had a small house and we moved into another, even smaller house. I was hanging out with my friend and she asked why I moved. I didn't know why we moved, but I knew that usually when people moved they moved into a bigger house. So I lied and told my friend we moved into a mansion. I never thought she'd see the house. But one day her mom dropped me off at my house, and she came inside and told my mom what I had said. My mom was like, 'Why did you tell them we lived in a mansion?' I couldn't explain it at the time, but now I think it's because I was embarrassed about living in a small house and didn't know why."

As I'm telling this story, I think about my daughter's friend who's always bragging about having an indoor pool, how she flies on a private jet, how her family is friends with Drake—who knows, maybe it's real. But there's definitely something going on with her if she feels the need to talk about it all the time. Because of this confusing financial pressure kids can sense, they sometimes need to lie about what they have. Especially with social media now—if I was lying to cope with what I didn't understand back in the day, I can only imagine how kids feel now, seeing kids with unbelievable lifestyles all over the internet.

All this reminds me of something that happened last winter.

Our youngest son walked downstairs wearing his older brother's old pants, which he'd ripped into shorts.

"What are you wearing!" my middle son laughed.

To be honest, I never think about buying my youngest son clothing—I always think, Hey, he has two older brothers, that's double the wardrobe! What I tend to blank on is that boys get holes, they skin their knees, and they cake their clothing in dirt.

So my sweet youngest son has taken to ripping pants at the knees where they're worn out to form shorts. Hand-me-downs create fashion visionaries!

"It's the new style, haven't you heard? Winter shorts!" my youngest hams it up for us, hands on hips like a fashion model.

Having multiple kids and trying to juggle your financial reality looks different for every family. In ours, the oldest kid gets dropped off at private school, where we line up with high-end sports cars, and the youngest kid is almost troublingly confident in his hand-me-down clothing. We can't help but laugh at it. As you become more comfortable as a parent, you gain wisdom, and realize that giving your kids things financially isn't what's most important. As long as everyone is fed, clothed, educated, and cared for, the rest is just gravy. What you can purchase with money isn't what matters. That being said, I did take my youngest to Old Navy after his fashion show because I'm starting to be weirded out by his Daisy Dukes.

# Nothing Like Joanna Gaines

**Confession:** *"There's a million fucking shows about making your space beautiful or perfectly organized. Then I go on Instagram and get all these ads for products for my home, and all these accounts are posting beautiful pictures of spotless houses. I look around my house, dirty dishes everywhere, shit everywhere, and feel like I'm failing at being the stylish, put-together mom I always wanted to be. I just wish that I could make my kids stop messing up the space, and I wish I could afford to get all the hundred-dollar throw pillows I see on Instagram!" –Anonymous*

My daughter and I love to bond over home decoration and renovation shows. Nat is not a fan, but for me and my daughter, there's something fulfilling about sitting on the couch with a big bowl of kettle corn and watching other people work really hard to totally transform a space. It's like a makeover show—satisfying to watch, and witnessing the transformation almost feels like you're accomplishing something. There's also something deeply stress-relieving about being able to give our own opinions on whether something's working, or rag on the choices they're making on the show without the burden of actually having to make any of those choices ourselves.

One night, after a particularly long binge session of *White Couple*

*Flips a House* (there are truly a ridiculous number of these shows), my daughter and I turn off the TV and look around. I notice her sigh. She says, "I wish our house looked like the TV houses." This makes me want to laugh and cry. The girl who can't do her dishes without groaning and dragging her feet wants an HGTV house? But also, I see her point. Suddenly, our home looks like a total pigsty. Where did all this shit come from! I don't remember buying so many mismatched socks, balls of slime, and lunch containers. Did it look like this when we sat down, or did some alien life-form (aka our family) come and throw everything around while we weren't looking? Did the carpets always clash with the ottoman? Was that hole in the wall next to the basement door always there?

We recently moved into a new house, and designing and putting the house together was a huge project. My dream was that before I moved into the new house, I'd purge everything I owned and enter the new house with a clean slate. But somehow, the more I purge, the more the stuff just keeps regenerating. It's like a reverse law of physics. The more you get rid of, the more you feel the need to buy. I look around every month and I swear on the shopping channel's grave that even though I didn't buy anything, there are more Tupperware lids with no matching bottoms than ever before. Like all moms on Instagram or Pinterest, I have this dream of being minimalist and clean. That if I just purchase the correct kind of bin, my kids will actually *want* to store their toys in it and tidy up after themselves. When we moved out of our last house, it felt like I spent an entire lifetime cleaning. Drawers, kitchen cupboards, under beds—how is it even possible for a family to have this many *items*?!

Minimalism is the trend du jour—everything has a perfect place and looks sleek, elegant, put together. These minimalist people seem to have two white T-shirts and one fork per family member; their homes have curated neutral items, and everything is pretty and handmade. You smell sandalwood and lavender just *looking at pictures* of minimalist houses. They fill me with such envy that I kinda hope someday one of them gets exposed with an Amazon package on their doorstep or a secret cupboard filled with clothes from high school and extra forks.

There are so many different versions of how to redo your home these days, it's hard to even pick an idea to stick to. There's the Marie Kondo method of course, which is throwing out or donating anything that doesn't "spark joy." With three kids, that is a tricky one. Does my son's PlayStation game where he shoots people's heads off really bring me joy? Do my husband's fifteen different biographies of old sports icons bring me joy? Not particularly, but I also can't just toss them.

Then there's Joanna Gaines, with her cute midcentury wood furniture, her perfectly sparse floral arrangements, her cream-and-neutral-toned palette—just the right amount of shabby chic. In the photos she posts, she's effortlessly icing a cake while her cute baby sits on the counter next to her, or walking into her expansive marble kitchen with a basket of freshly picked fruit from the fruit tree she has outside. Meanwhile, I'm slicing up a frozen pizza with three kids yelling at me from different points in the house, picking something sticky out of my hair, and trying not to spill pizza grease on my kid's homework, which they've left, for some reason, on the stove?

Next we have The Home Edit, a home-organizing brand that has a different take than Marie Kondo. Their philosophy is more like "Buy whatever the fuck you want—buy tons of stuff!—and we'll figure out a way to organize it all by color in clear bins. It'll look pristine, never mind that it might not actually be 'practical.' Oh, and it will be like, $200/hr to organize, or you can do it yourself if you buy about 1,000 of our $30 plastic bins."

I'm lying in bed that night after watching the *White Couple Flips a House* TV show with my daughter, and her words are haunting me. Why doesn't our house look like the houses on TV? We'd literally just moved, and I spent so much time trying to make it look perfect. I thought out what their bedrooms would look like, I made a cool bathroom, I even designed a room at the front of the house where only two people can sit so I can have one-on-one time with my family members while telling anyone who intrudes that there's simply no room. And while that doesn't stop all the kids from piling onto the two armchairs in there, the intention should count for something.

I go downstairs to get some water, and with all the lights off in the house, I slide on markers that are, for some reason, covering the kitchen floor. I land on my ass with a THUD and yell. Okay, this is the LAST STRAW. I'm getting this house organized if it kills me—and I'd rather a clean house kill me than these fucking markers. I go back upstairs, open up my laptop, and enter an Amazon-fueled fever dream. I'm frantically searching for different organizational storage containers. I start a document with a list of options. There's one that stacks white squares, there's one that's clear, there's one that's like bamboo or something. There are so many options. I open Joanna Gaines's Instagram. Which one would she pick? Is there one where my kids get candy every time they put shit back in the compartments? We need incentives, people! Clearly these were not designed by parents living in reality.

My husband walks into the bedroom and I show him my spreadsheet of potential organizational tools. It'll be life-changing, I say to him, just imagine everything put away in neat little containers! I'm arguing like a lawyer fighting the case of my life here, like I *know* if we just buy a *few more things*, our house will be perfect. If I can just be influenced by the right influencer, our house will be spotless. My husband laughs and shakes his head. He knows this fevered desire for order won't last. Usually it's him who's the neat freak. See, my theory is there is always one partner who is a neat freak, because two neat freaks cannot survive children. My husband would have this house so organized, but I am a disaster (I like to say I'm responsible for the fun). It's like the harder I try to be organized, the worse it gets. He's like, "CAT, just put shit away!!" And I'm like, "My brain doesn't work like that!" He's like, "Stop buying shit!!" I'm like, "It will help me!!" Then I try for like a week to really be organized and fail after week one and go back to chasing my tail. And this dance has gone on and on since we got married. He would be Joanna Gaines. He has his socks matching. It boggles my mind.

"You've been watching HGTV again, haven't you?" he says.

Is it that obvious? He shuts my laptop.

"Have you ever considered," he says, while encouraging me to drink my glass of water, bringing me out of my online shopping fugue state, "that the houses on those shows aren't lived in?

Imagine going back to those houses two months after the TV crews leave. Do you think they'd still look like that? No way. They probably have shit and crayon markings on the walls. Recycling bins overflowing. You're comparing our home to a house that no one lives in!"

He's so right. My mind is comparing this home that's overflowing with love and rowdy, sometimes annoying living creatures to a house with staged furniture and an arsenal of professional designers. How absurd is that?

The next day, I get home from grocery shopping and I'm so exhausted, running through my list of what's left to do that night. I'm picturing a quick dinner with the kids, then a loooong, hot shower. When I come into the house, there's a trail of pillowcases, colored paper, and what looks like actual crumbs. Like I'm some sort of witch following Hansel and Gretel's trail.

I walk into the living room. It looks like a Bed Bath & Beyond exploded up in here. Sheets hung from the light fixtures I painstakingly chose. My good throw cushions being smushed beyond recognition.

My kids have made a fort. It looks hideous, made with stained old bedsheets and hilariously precariously placed blankets. You would not pin this image on Pinterest. My first thought is how long this is going to take me to clean up once they get bored of it and return to their rooms to play video games. But I take a beat, then crawl in, and my three sweet kids are in there together, laughing hysterically over a fart joke. In that moment, I don't care that the living room is a disaster and dinner is definitely going to have to be from the freezer again. In this moment, what I need is to soak up this time with my kids.

They're so proud of this imaginary world they've made together, and so excited to show it to me. I act awed by their architecture, the way they've managed to balance the pillows, the little windows they've constructed between the blanket folds, their ingenious use of the ottoman. They've created a whole little world out of furniture I bought with the intention of it looking beautiful. I never anticipated it would be used for this kind of purpose, but this is so much better than an Instagram photo. I'll even ignore, just for this evening, that they're wiping their chip-greased hands all over my beautiful rug.

The desire to have a perfectly organized home space is really the desire for control in a chaotic life. I'll probably never stop trying to organize my home. But I don't want little robot children who are scared I'll flip out at them for leaving their socks on the ground *again*. I like my little den of wildlings, even if it means I might never have the home photo shoot of my dreams. Home trends come and go, but this ugly little fort and all the other spontaneous fun we have together? That's what really makes a home.

# ELEVEN

# Not Like Other Girls

**Confession:** *"For some reason, I have a hard time keeping women as friends. Sometimes I worry that I just don't get along with other women. I have a tendency to gossip, and I feel like that's ruined some friendships for me. I don't know why I do it, but hating on other women is easier for me than trying to be friends with them. But I really feel like I'm missing out, and just don't understand why I don't have a girl gang to hang out with." –Anonymous*

Hi, confessor. You have come to the right place with this one. As, like, the patron saints of girlfriends, we're about to give you some tough love: the reason you don't have a girl gang to hang out with is because you're hating on other women. And the reason you're hating on other women is that you've been taught that it's an okay way to deal with your own insecurities—that putting other women down will make you feel better. The good news? You recognize it's a problem and you want to fix it. The better news? We can help you do that!

We've heard confessions like this time and time again, and it pains us every time. A woman will say to us, "I don't get along with other girls. I just don't find women that easy to get along with." This comes from women we respect, women we like and are friends with. And when we hear it, we feel like they're seeing the world through a lens that is so, so limited. They're not getting to experience and benefit from what could be one of the most amazing relationships in their lifetime, which is true friendship with another woman. We feel sad for people who tell us that, and we wish we could tell them they have it all wrong. Because you know who has supported us in our business, given us free advice and consultations, and offered a helping hand in whatever way they can? Other women.

In a female friendship, something magical happens. We always say there should be just as much, if not more, emphasis on your best friend as there is on your marriage or relationship with your significant other. Your best friend doesn't want anything from you, not the way a partner wants kids, or dinner, or sex—or any of the other myriad needs of a romantic relationship. Which are all great in their own way and in their own time. But your best friend is just there to talk, to complain to, to cry with, to pour some more wine and yell about something totally off-color just to make you laugh.

Having a group of best friends is also amazing—having multiple women's perspectives and advice is fabulous. As women, we're conditioned to think it's not possible to have a group of women get together and be there for each other without some element of jealousy or competitiveness entering the mix. That if a bunch of women are hanging out, there's some backdoor gossip or shit-talking that happens. Culturally, we're shown that example over and over again. It's in every movie, TV show, internet drama. But if you're confident in yourself, and secure in yourself, you realize that having fun and supporting your friends is so much more fun and interesting than speaking badly of them to make yourself feel better. A lot of people blame gossip, hurtful actions, and drama on others, but it's important to really reflect and consider what energy you're bringing to a group dynamic. If you can let your ego go, let your walls down, and accept yourself and all your flaws, you'll find that bringing other women into the fold is such a joy. And when we can be kind to ourselves, we understand that we need to give ourselves a break, and we give others a break, too.

Where does this idea that women are naturally competitive and jealous of each other come from? It comes from a scarcity mind-set. The mind-set that there isn't a place at the table for all of us. That if one woman succeeds, it means you will fail. Which is simply not true! It's a mind-set that was created back when it seemed like women had to fight each other tooth and nail for a seat at the table. Because men wouldn't let us have one! Thankfully, we're now entering an era where women have secured a lot of those seats at the table, and they're working hard to make room for others of all identities to have power, security, and all the opportunities they want, too. We need to shift to an abundance mind-set instead of a scarcity mind-set. An abundance mind-set is realizing that the more other women succeed, the more you will succeed. And that if other women help you and you turn around and help other women, there's just more to go around all over. Changing that narrative in your head doesn't happen overnight. This idea of fear and possessiveness, of tearing down the girls around you, is baked into us at a young age. And if you learn it young and never grow out of it, it can really poison your friendships.

Our daughters' teachers have told us that there's a lot of drama in junior high (not that they needed to tell us—we were once tween girls too), and that a lot of girls pick fights for no reason. But we know the reason: these girls are young, they're figuring out their identities, and they're scared of being made fun of. Our daughters' schools ask incoming students what their biggest concerns are, and half the class of eleven-year-old girls said their biggest concern is what they look like. That's astounding, and heartbreaking. Even girls with the most loving home environments arrive at middle school with the idea that their waistline determines their popularity. And girls who are picking fights or causing drama aren't bad girls or bad kids!! They're just feeling insecure, and trying to be popular, and haven't been given the tools or coping skills to feel secure in their social situation without tearing other people down.

Have you ever heard a girl claim they're "not like other girls," or heard a guy say this to a girl in a way that was supposed to be a compliment? (Have you ever managed to let them finish that sentence without rolling your eyes so hard, you get a glimpse of your brain? We haven't.) When we hear people say they're "not like other girls," we want to say, "Oh really? I'm totally like other girls. Other girls are fucking amazing." Why should we allow men (or other women, for that matter) to insult womanhood as a whole? Do we do it to make ourselves feel unique? Here's a secret:

we're all unique! Even if you like HGTV and red wine and Taylor Swift! Jesus fucking Christ. Can we just let women enjoy things and still recognize we're worthwhile human beings? Think about the progress we could make if we all flipped the script that way. If we taught our kids not to get caught up in that backhanded compliment. Mothers, parents, mentors—we set the tone for our daughters and kids. We're their role models for how to behave in various situations, and they take those actions to heart. They will likely even repeat those actions themselves, because they trust us.

But let's say you're the most amazing role model of all time. You're still not the only influence on your kid. We've seen it play out so many times: a huge topic of conversation between women is the flaws of other women. It's creepy: you see this between adult women, and then you see the parallel conversation between young girls. Our kids get into these conversations about female celebrities: "Which one is better?" "Which one is prettier?" "Who is cooler?" And we have to wonder, why is this comparison not made between the boy celebrities? One of our mom friends once said, "I hate this TikTok girl," and we had to stop and ask, "Why are you, a grown adult woman, passing judgment on this teenage girl?" As moms, we need to de-escalate these conversations when they arise, and really think about what's behind them.

When our daughters talk about someone at school they don't like, it's a balancing act. You don't want to invalidate their feelings, and you want to hear them out if they're having a hard time. But when we hear them slip into speaking poorly about one of their friends, we like to remind our kids that we don't talk about friends like that. In a gentle but firm way, we just remind them that if we've had them over to our house, we've invited them into our intimate lives, and we're not going to speak ill of them unless there's a real conflict to be resolved. Setting that standard and tone is important. It's important to us not to accept this idea of "Hey, we can take each other down a peg and speak ill of each other, it's fun and it's cool, it's morally okay," because it's not! And all those small instances of that add up.

Recently, one of our daughters had an experience where one of her friends was talking badly about another friend (there's three of them, which is always tricky). The friend was texting my daughter, saying "I don't like this girl" and speaking poorly of her without any real reason to—other than, probably, to try to strengthen her bond with my daughter. My daughter wasn't sure what to do, and my advice to her was to respond to this girl that she likes both of them, she's friends with them both. And don't get into the rest of the drama. The girl didn't know what to say back to this—she just said, "Oh, okay," and ended it nicely. It's likely she was feeling insecure, but once my daughter reassured her that she liked them both, it cut the drama from the interaction.

Our other daughter had a similar situation happen. She came to me and said she needed help responding to a text—there was a fight going on and she didn't know how to end it, but just wanted it to end. She asked me for help, which was very mature of her. My approach was to advise her to say something that would defuse the situation, not encourage the argument and conversation. We did that, and then it was over, and the conversation was never brought up again. As adults, we have the tools to know how to de-escalate a situation. I'm sure my daughter will remember the time she was able to craft a text that ended a fight instead of escalating it into bigger drama. But kids don't always bring this kind of thing to you. It's important to reach out to them preemptively. Ask them, How are things going with the girls? Bring up the girls! Don't assume nothing is happening just because they haven't brought anything up. Ask if the girls are being kind to each other, or if there are any issues. They might start opening up, and they might need help!

Kudos to every woman who shows up and helps another woman out without asking for anything in return. That's the real story of women. We're fed this toxic, women-hating-women, gossipy, jealous narrative of female friendship, but more often than not, it's just not true. There are far more positive stories we don't hear about. A woman doing something for another woman she cares about will never ask for a thank-you or for attention—it won't make the news or go viral. She'll do it because she cares.

We see moms in our community line up around the block with food whenever another mom in our community is going through a hard time. We see moms helping a mom they don't know load groceries into her car. We see moms fund-raise, organize, protest, cook, clean, work—all without asking for recognition. And maybe we should really start highlighting *that*. Even something as simple as seeing a woman praise another woman on social media makes you feel good! Because at our core, we want to lift each other up. We've been clouded by so many things. Judgment, guilt, self-loathing, insecurity. Oh, and definitely men. Don't forget the men, it's always their fault. (Kidding.) (Sort of.) But don't let those things rob you of friendships that will change your life.

# TWELVE

# Negotiating with the Tooth Fairy

*Nat*

**Confession:** *"I'm getting really tired of pretending to be magical beings for my kids. It may have been fun and easy at first, but it's year after year and I'm getting to a point where I'm messing up and forgetting things and they're starting to catch on. I'm not sure how I can stop without crushing their imaginations, but also don't know what the right age is to tell them the sad, boring truth."* –Anonymous

There comes a time in every child's life when they become suspicious of the magic their parents have been carefully spoonfeeding them their whole lives. Depending on how you decide to raise your kids, you may or may not follow certain cultural scripts around magical beings and happenings. You might encourage them to believe in these things, even making up family traditions around them. Whether your kid is obsessed with finding fairies in the trees in the backyard or thinks the Elf on the Shelf is his best friend, it's hard to know at what age it's appropriate to tell them the harsh reality: that while there are many wonderful and interesting things about life, hippogriffs are just fiction (and on that note, they're a boring Muggle kid who won't be getting their letter of acceptance by owl when they turn eleven).

Who wants to be the person to spoil the magical feelings and expansive imaginations our kids have? Do you crush your kid's sparkly magical dreams now, or do they hate you later on when they realize you've been lying to them? I mean, is there anything wrong with having an adult child who believes in unicorns? And sometimes, it's not just a simple binary of believing versus not believing.

As you know by now, Cat and I have seven kids between us. Take that, and multiply it by twenty. That's one hundred and forty baby teeth. When you have a lot of kids around the tooth-losing age, it seems like you have to be prepared for a tooth to straight up fall out of your kid's mouth out at any minute, seemingly unprompted. It can happen literally anywhere, but it's never at the *right* time. I can't tell you how many times I've been minding my own business when my child has come up to me, hands cupping a bloody tooth, desperate to show me the fleshy gum it's just come out of. Maybe that's why the tooth fairy was invented—as a kid, it's pretty creepy for your teeth to just keep falling out of your mouth, but nothing mitigates weirdness like a cash bonus. The more teeth fall out, the more money you get. Did a child business mogul invent this shit? I feel like the grown-ups are being swindled.

Last night the tooth fairy forgot to come for my son's tooth. And it was a front tooth, so, like, it was a big deal. I realize at breakfast that I forgot, but I try to cover it up by playing coy. "Did the tooth fairy come last night?" I ask him. He says, "Mom, you know the tooth fairy didn't come." Okay, I guess he's onto me. He's my middle son, and it's a tricky balance—his younger brother and some of his friends still believe, so I end up feeling murky about what page he's on. Sometimes I think the kids hold on to the belief even when, deep down, they already know better. I can't blame them for holding on to that piece of childhood. But when

Cat's oldest daughter wouldn't cop to knowing that Santa isn't real, Cat's mother said, "Cat, I think it's time she learns about the tooth fairy and Santa. She knows about sex, after all." And we couldn't disagree! At that point, Cat and her daughter sat down together and mutually agreed to acknowledge that Santa isn't real, but that they'd keep up the ruse for the younger siblings.

To make matters worse, it always takes me a week or so after a tooth falls out to remember to sneak something under the pillow. In my time as the tooth fairy, I've been able to develop a repertoire of excuses for why the tooth fairy is late or didn't bother to show at all. "Oh, honey, it's really bad weather, she couldn't fly here in time, she wasn't feeling well I heard, too many kids have lost teeth, she's sooo busy!" It's to the point now where my kids think flakiness is just part of the tooth fairy's personality.

But now that my son knows it's me, not the tooth fairy, who keeps flaking on him, I feel more motivated to make sure he doesn't lose faith in me as well. While he's at school and I'm working from home, I search the house high and low and, wouldn't you know it, not a dollar to be found. (On mom blogs and Facebook groups, you'll see a smattering of posts about how much coin to give per tooth. A quarter, a dollar? Are we supposed to be keeping up with inflation? Is this, like, for their college fund or their candy fund? My take: It's whatever you have lying around.)

All I can find before I have to jump on a call is a $100 US bill left over from either when I was on tour with Cat or my trip to Florida in 1995. Well, maybe I'll just tell him that if the tooth fairy is late, you grow interest. And the tooth fairy didn't have time to exchange her currency on her way over. Lucky kid!

Middle children have it the hardest, we think. They aren't quite as sheltered as the youngest, but they aren't as world-weary as the oldest. As a result, they kind of go back and forth between what they believe in. After school that same day, my ten-year-old, who had just said all-knowingly that he knew *I* knew "the tooth fairy" didn't come, shocks me. He comes home all psyched and is like, "MOM, GUESS WHAT! My friend got footage of the tooth fairy on his phone! He caught the tooth fairy flying around!" So you don't believe in the tooth fairy at home, but you believe in the tooth fairy at your friend's house? It seems cruel to point out this obvious contradiction, but I just keep my mouth shut and hope his critical-thinking skills improve by the time he's in high school.

My husband gives me a side-eye when our son comes downstairs the next morning with a $100 US bill. I tell him to take it up with the tooth fairy.

THIRTEEN

# Marriage Advice from Our Stripper

**Confession:** *"I am going to shave my partner's head in their sleep if they forget to unload the dishwasher one more time. No one fucking prepares you for marriage! I love my partner, but it's not like . . . teenage love, or even engagement or pre-kids-married-life love . . . and I feel bad for saying that, because every day some twenty-five-year-old on Instagram is expressing his intense love for his girlfriend. Do I just need to like, buy some lingerie like in the movies? What's my problem?"* –Anonymous

t's Friday night. Our husbands have taken the kids to a movie night, and we have Nat's house to ourselves. Which means the rosé is flowing, and it's time to talk shit and gripe without having to hide in a closet from our kids. (Just kidding.) (Except about the rosé.) Now that the kids are a bit older, we've actually been having some good one-on-one time that's not impeded by a constant scramble of emergency kid needs. With the kids out of the crisis baby stage, we have time to actually think about ourselves, deeply, for the first time in . . . years? This time to think is fun—we've been able to rank members of the royal family based on relatability (thank you, Princess Charlotte, for the win there), plan the trips we're going to take once our kids are out of the house (husbands not invited, obviously), and work on our business (this one isn't funny, but as working moms, it's important).

But it's also . . . terrifying. Suddenly, we actually have the mental capacity to *reflect*. And what good ever came from being emotionally intelligent and introspective?! We've been having a lot of nights like this, reflecting on things together and digging into topics we honestly just haven't had the mental capacity to even entertain for the past decade or so. This thinking, of course, includes a huge part of our lives: our marriages.

This Friday night, we're chatting, laughing, I'm scrolling through Instagram to show Nat this hilarious meme, when suddenly, a post from one of the male strippers that we take on tour with us pops up. It's an all-text post that reads: "Statistics show that 50% of marriages end in divorce. The other 50% break down like this: 2% reach success with ultimate love & happiness. 3% still have romance with lil' ups and downs but can maintain. The 45% left are stuck in an unhappy situation . . . they're trapped and can't get out . . . they gotta stay in it for financial reasons, kids, or to make it look good for family and friends." Underneath he includes that emoji with the eyebrows raised way up, eyeballs popping out. Pretty much my face while I'm reading it.

Nat's like, "What's the deal?" I turn my phone to her. She reads it and, without saying anything, immediately stands to get more wine. Who knew our stripper friend was going to send us into an existential tailspin?!

Glasses topped up, she comes back.

"You know," I say to her, "I'm really challenging the theory of marriage these days. Not because I want a divorce, not at all.

But because I need to wrap my head around what we did as young twentysomethings. Think about all the stupid stuff we did. Like that time we invited that random guy from the laundromat to my parents' anniversary party. Or the time we left chicken nuggets in the hot oven all night because we forgot about them and fell asleep. The same girls who did that idiotic shit somehow also chose partners for life."

"You know what," Nat says emphatically, "I commend us and our twentysomething selves for *finding* these men! When we had small kids, I didn't even have time to stop and think about my marriage. I was too busy washing poo off my shirt and trying to stop my toddler from accidentally buying more apps on my iPhone. And that's lucky, that the marriage could just be in the background, supporting us. But now that the kids are older, I've really been thinking about, like, what *is* this marriage now? Not in a way that's even explicitly about our husbands, but just about the institution of marriage itself. What we got ourselves into! No one told me so many things about marriage. No one told me we'd be in a pandemic together! Things get hard, and it's like, 'I guess we just keep going.'"

"Yeah," I say, taking a sip of wine. "You know, my husband is sometimes in my space a lot . . . but overall, for the fact that I have to live with an adult man every single day, he's a pretty great team member. That's what marriage can feel like a lot of the time. I'm with him all the time. As a mature married girl"—I'm always a girl, never a woman—"we make good, solid partnership decisions. They don't talk about that in *The Notebook*! It's so unromantic!"

"Yeah," Nat replies. "When you have a family, you need support. You need a teammate. The romance in that one-on-one way can come in a different way when the kids are a bit more grown. But we have three, four kids and a dog whose lives we have to maneuver every single day. I do not have time to date my husband—that's why he's a husband!"

It's a lot to consider, this fairy-tale notion of "happily ever after" that's sold to us as children, all lifelong rose petals and candlelight. But what happens after the credits roll on the rom-coms? Is this Instagram statistic our fate? And is that a bad thing? I stand up to get another glass of wine, and my back seizes up.

"You know," I say to Nat, "this weekend was the first weekend *ever* that I've raked leaves. And I fucking *hated* it. I couldn't walk for three days because I was so sore from bending over and raking! My husband is the one who does all the outside shit. It's one of those things that you barely even think of when you're not the one doing it. But then I did it once, and God, I am so thankful he takes care of all that. After doing it, I was like, 'Okay, fair. Good. Yeah, you do this stuff for me, and I do things for you.' It's a good balance. Sharing the workload, division of labor."

"Yeah. The stuff of life that is soooo boring is shared, but no one ever talks about that! Imagine doing all of it yourself! God bless single parents! But . . . let's also get this straight—it's not like I *can't* rake the leaves or need a man to do it for me. I'm not some delicate flower, although my back might beg to differ. It's just nice to not have to worry about it—to trust that someone else will cover that side of things."

There's a fantasy about love and marriage that we definitely had when we were younger, and you think that things are going to stay that way forever. That you'll be able to devote so much time and attention to your partner, and to yourself, and that when you have a slew of tiny human beings around you, nothing will change. But that's not realistic! You have mouths to feed, you have so many needs, so many dynamics to juggle. And so little privacy . . . as in, none.

Nat reads my mind and says, "People think if you're in love with your partner, you have to be in movie love, Instagram love. Every anniversary or birthday or time he takes out the trash, you're supposed to be like, 'You're my everything! Couldn't live without you, babe! My rock, my hero, my soulmate.'" Nat rolls her eyes. Gag!

"We've been taught," I say, "as girls and as women, that we need men, and men have been taught that women need them, so they're always in a position of power over us. It shouldn't be that we *need* them, or are *forced* to have them, but that it's a choice. That's what I tell my husband all the time, and he used to get offended, but now he takes it as a compliment. 'I *choose* you, I don't *need* you.' That's a good thing. That's even more romantic—it's an active decision to be together. I once heard that every fight comes from an expectation that wasn't met, so it's based on your expectations that someone lets you down. Your expectations are not necessarily reality. Expectations change, life changes. You change!"

You know, we've both been married for over thirteen years. That's a *really* long time. Think of how much you changed as a human between the ages of thirteen and twenty-six. Or twenty-six and thirty-nine. Your marriage evolves, too, and we now have a new appreciation for it, a new understanding. It gets really hard for a while, there's growing pains. You settle in, you make a choice, like, "Okay, I guess we're going to do this!" You'd think that choice is just made at the altar, but really it comes much later, and it comes again and again and again. It comes at three a.m. when your baby is crying, it comes when leaves are piling up on your driveway, it comes when you need someone to come with you to an awful, boring work event.

Nat quiets for a second. Then she says, "Cat, do you believe in soul mates?"

I think about what we've just been discussing, and how your life partner is a choice you make over and over again, not some random person you're "destined" to be with. "Meh . . ."

"Maybe with friendships?" we both say at once. We die laughing. As we probably will until we actually die, decades later, retired and old and wrinkly and together, probably still gossiping over rosé.

# FOURTEEN

# Sex Ed for Dummies

**Confession:** *"My daughter (16) was caught giving or getting (I didn't want to know which) oral to (or from?) her boyfriend by his mom. The mom called me and filled me in, which was awkward AF. My husband and I called our daughter to our room immediately and attempted some sort of conversation that was nice and not shaming but also stern. It was awkward and horrifying for all involved. I have no idea if we did a good job."* –Anonymous

It's the Saturday night before my daughter starts middle school. I'm ready. I got her ten different color-coded binders, her pencil case is ready to go, I even got her a cute mirror to stick in her locker during a late-night Amazon prime binge and *Saved by the Bell*–era nostalgia wave. But somewhere between almost buying her a pen with a fuzzy pom-pom on top and asking her if she needs more socks, I forgot—or realistically, maybe I'd just been avoiding thinking about—the *other* part of middle school. The nonacademic part. The part that involves mixed-gender dances and braces-to-braces kissing. Blah. I look over at my beautiful daughter, who says she does need new socks, and feel the motherly panic build.

After an anxious late-night Google deep dive, I find a Reddit thread covering all the things everyone thinks you should tell your kids before they reach puberty. Some are proponents of the "tell all" method (porn, marijuana, Four Loko—you name it, they've discussed it), while others are vehemently on the side of a sort of "don't ask, don't tell" approach. I spend an hour reading back-and-forth comments between SoccerMom101 and ChristianDad113, with brief appearances by 123KittyLover, who's got some wack shit going on, and decide I am a failure as a parent in every single way.

After a restless night imagining my daughter not knowing what an Eiffel Tower is and embarrassing herself in front of everyone, I go over to Cat's house and tell her I'm trying to come up with The List. You know, a quick-and-easy rundown of Everything My Daughter Needs to Know Before Middle School. Simple, right?

We're both at a bit of a loss here. "She knows how babies are made, she knows smoking is bad, what else are you going to talk to her about?" Cat asks me. ". . . *Fingering?*"

"I DON'T KNOW! I GUESS!" I yell.

Should I tell her about fingering? What is the right amount of information to give one's child about fingering? And are we talking about fingering yourself? Or others fingering you? Is that too much of a leap, when only a few years ago I convinced her the correct word for "vagina" was "wageena" because I thought she sounded so cute when she said it? You have such a finite window to get everything in their brains before the train leaves the station, and I don't even know where to put any type of fingering on that list.

Then there's the question of whether I should even broach the subject at all. Middle school, junior high, whatever you might call it, is the strangest two years of a young person's life. The sun is going down on childhood, and yet there's still so much innocence. You may have boobs and hair on your genitals, but you can't drink, smoke, or use your orifices for anything really fun. This limbo is like a Bermuda Triangle for new, awkward, confusing experiences, and there's only so much we as parents can do to shield them from certain information. You only have total control over the information your kids are getting for so long before they starting getting it somewhere else, whether that's some random account they stumble across on the internet or the asshole boy at school. The short of it is, whatever you're not telling them yourself, they're going to find out about from someone else, and you have to decide where your boundaries are with that.

With children, the easiest way to approach the topic of sex is to describe the heteronormative 1950s version of a sex life. Chaste, Sunday school–approved, endorsed by grandmothers everywhere. Think rose petals strewn on silk bedsheets on your wedding night, genitals referred to as flowers. It's easy to explain because it's sanitized, functional, practical, reproductive: You're in love, you get married, penis goes into vagina one time and results in a baby. Then you never do it again.

But what if my daughter goes to school on Monday and sweet little Suzy from around the block starts talking at recess about how she got fingered at summer camp, and my daughter knows they definitely don't love each other and aren't married and doesn't think that finger in vagina makes a baby. Then where do we go with that?

Cat and I decide to do some role-playing (oh God—do I have to explain role-playing?!) to figure out how to explain these mysterious human behaviors to our kids. We sit together on the couch and Cat pretends to be my daughter as we rehearse this. I compose myself, trying to look like a chill, sex-positive Cool Mom.

Think Lorelai from *Gilmore Girls* if she had finally kicked the coffee addiction.

"Okay, sweetie, so there are a few things I want to talk to you about before middle school starts."

"Mooooom," Cat says, doing an excellent tween impression, "I just want to go practice my TikTok dance, I'm bored." I try not to laugh.

"Well, honey, let's just have a super-quick chat. I know we've talked about sex before—"

"EWWW!"

"—but there are a few . . . other . . . kinds of sex we should talk about just in case it comes up at school."

"Other kinds of sex? There are different kinds?"

"Well, I guess they're kind of all the same kind. Different parts of the same kind? Like how there's both ice cream and gelato and like, Popsicles, I guess?" I break character for a moment. "Cat, am I making any sense?"

"Yes, keep going, this is great, I'm an enthralled twelve-year-old."

"Okay, well, so first of all, there's this thing called a blow job . . ." Cat is already laughing at me but I try to power through. ". . . and so it's kind of like . . . sometimes when you love someone, and they have a penis, you might want to put it in your mouth . . ."

"EW! Mom, that's disgusting, why would they do that?!"

"Well, sweetie, that's an incredible question. Actually, I don't know why we do it . . . I wonder about that a lot. I guess when I . . . when Mommy and Daddy—no, too weird. Remember those characters in *Hotel Transylvania* that like each other? I mean, pleasure is . . . Shit, how do I even answer that?"

I'm about to say that "sometimes Mommy needs to be nice to Daddy but she doesn't feel like putting the penis into the vagina and a blow job is much more efficient," but I try to keep it together to get to the main event.

"Let's step aside from the blow job thing for a sec, might be too advanced. Another thing that might be good to know in case anyone talks about it is this thing called fingering."

"That sounds painful! What is it?"

"So basically, it's this thing where someone puts their fingers in your vagina . . ."

"EW! That's so gross! Like a tampon? Does it hurt? Why would they do that?"

"Well, first of all, never let ANYONE do that unless you explicitly ask them to, and if anyone ever does it to you without asking you first, you come to me and I'll kill them. But back to why . . . it can feel good, actually, but if they're not good at it, it can also feel really bad . . . but still good in a weird way?" We both start laughing uncontrollably.

"And Mom," Cat says, back in her role, "do you do this?" She gives me big innocent-child eyes.

I break character and say to Cat, "Oh my God, is this going horribly? Am I a bad mother? How on earth do I explain this? Is she too young?"

Even as we're role-playing, I am unsure if it's best for my kids to hear about all the weird-yet-pleasurable stuff we can do with our bodies from me. Especially when I don't want to encourage them to be having sex until they're older.

After another round of acting out the Sex Talk, I make a

decision. I'm going to tell my daughter a *version* of fingering. A version of sex ed, and I'll determine what's included in that version when she feels it's a good time to ask me about it. For now, as she embarks on the new frontier of middle school, filled as it is with dick drawings and fart jokes, I'll tell her that in the next few years, there might be things that come up that are new, that she hasn't heard of before. And that's very normal. And that if she ever wants to talk to me about it, I'm here for her to talk to, no matter how weird she might think it is. I want to talk to her about it, no questions asked. And she can always go to Cat, too, if it seems too gross to ask her own mom.

But until then, I have to ask myself the question: What's more traumatizing, not knowing what fingering is when Suzy tells you about it at recess and having to google it on your cell phone in the bathroom later, or your mother giving you an in-depth explanation of it? She may never take me (or Cat) up on the offer, but she knows it stands.

# FIFTEEN

# Cracking the Code of Your Kids' Texts

**Confession:** *"I gave my kid a phone so that we could communicate better when we're apart, but it seems like it's only made the communication more weird. Texting with a twelve-year-old is beyond annoying. Sometimes I hardly even understand what he's trying to say—and god FORBID I just call him. I often feel like I'm tryna talk to an alien. Any tweenage translators out there?" –Anonymous*

## NAT

Cat and I sometimes do guest appearances on TV segments or radio shows. These are always fun experiences—we get to talk to live audiences, chat about parenting and all our typical wildness and nonsense. One day we were on one of these shows that we'd been psyched for. We're partway through recording when my phone wouldn't stop vibrating. I'd left it in my pocket like a total TV novice, unlike the poised television expert I actually am. If it had been one call, then fine, we ignore it. But it legit vibrated fifteen times within ten minutes. The fifteenth time, I'm like, "Okay, I'm sorry but as per the reason we're on this show, I'm a mom and so I need to check who's calling me. A little behind-the-scenes parenting action! Just pretend we're in a documentary or something."

It was my daughter. I walk off the set and call her back.

"Hey sweetie, what's happened?"

She sounds distraught. She's eleven and just started at a new school, where she didn't really know anyone. I'm like oh God, what could've happened? Did she get bullied? Is she getting kicked out of school for bullying someone else? No, she'd never do that. But it must be something dire for her to call me this much. Did she flunk a test? Did she tell the principal to fuck off? (Which I'd support, he probs deserved it.)

"Mom, I don't have a fork for my lunch."

She doesn't have a fork for her lunch. Fifteen calls, and she doesn't have a fork for her lunch.

Have I failed in teaching my daughter to problem-solve? And this famous show we're on has just stopped recording, because why? Because my daughter doesn't have a fork. No, actually, it's because my daughter has a phone.

## CAT

Communication with preteens, tweens, teenagers, whatever you want to call them, is notoriously difficult. What they mean and what they know is constantly changing, and they grow so fast that it's sometimes hard to track where they're at. When they're a kid, Maslow's Hierarchy of Needs makes total sense. First, they need food, water, and shelter. Then they need safety and security. Love, etc.

As a teen, the hierarchy is more like: a shirt Charli D'Amelio wore, a text back from their crush, a Frappuccino, and then, out of nowhere, your complete undivided love and attention. It's hard to understand when they want space and when they want affection. And now, in our day and age, that communication is mediated by cell phones. Which you may think would assist with communication, but are often more of a hindrance than a help. There are many hoops to jump through and things to learn about texting with our offspring. We'll let you in on some of the things we've learned in the hopes that they might guide you when trekking into the unknown world of emojis and GIFs.

## The Solitary Hey

One thing to note is that kids never ask for what they want right away. You know a big ask is coming when they drop a solitary "hey" or "Mom?" You're like, okay, here we go. What's coming. And if it were something simple like "Can you order me lunch?" they would just text that. When there's an introduction, when they're trying to get your attention with a single word before the bomb drops, it's like, okay, back up, I need space, we have to prepare for this.

## The Fine Line Between Laughing and Crying

It's important to remember that tweens are experiencing everything for the first time, so every social interaction is really important to them. Even if you think it's dumb, like they forgot part of their costume for school-Halloween, or they want to go to a boy-girl Starbucks outing, for them it's big.

When they tell you about these situations over text, it's pretty much impossible to tell if they think what's just happened is soul-crushing or funny. My daughter will text me, "I got pranked at school today." Okay, so are we crying? Are we laughing? I'm gearing up to conduct an emergency therapy session like I'm a therapy bot: This is just what teen boys do. They're just trying to be naughty, but you're amazing and they probably just want your attention. Damage control. As I'm typing, she responds, "It's so funny they did it to everyone!" Sigh of relief.

## A Cell Phone Does Not Equal Freedom

A text message does not absolve all sins. Recently I was outside the school at three p.m. waiting to pick up my preteen daughter. She texted, "Hey! I'm going to hang out with my friend after school, be home later." It's like, dude, I have two other children, the world does not revolve around you! But she doesn't yet understand that while a phone is a way to communicate, it's not a superpower. It doesn't mean you just get to inform your mom of what you're doing.

Teens see phones as a replacement for permission. They're confusing the freedom to communicate with the freedom to do what they want. Even if you don't give them permission for something, they'll say, Oh, but I texted you! We have to drill it in that that's not how phones work. A text conversation is still a conversation. It's a two-way street. I have to respond and give you permission.

## The Ambiguous Bomb

And then, they can drop huge topics on you in the most casual way. Everything becomes so condensed and ambiguous over text. One day, my daughter was in health class, and she texted me, "Mom, what's birth control?" My first thought is, "If you're in health class, aren't they teaching you this? Why are you texting me?" My next thought is, "This is too big a conversation to have over text."

Then she texts me, "Can you send me some videos? I want to learn more about it." She wants to learn more about birth control? Why, is she going to have sex after school and needs to figure out her contraception? I mean, I know in my heart of hearts that the situation isn't that intense, but where is this coming from? They send you these ambiguous text messages and it's like solving a murder mystery.

It's amazing that our phones let us maintain a line of communication with our kids throughout the day, but it's also important to know where to set some boundaries. One of our friends has this app on her kid's phone that lets her track where her kid is at all times. This app is more common than you'd think.

My daughter, the same one sending the most ambiguous texts of all time, has recently started saying she wants me to put that tracker on her phone. She's terrified that when she becomes a real teen, she's going to get in all sorts of trouble. I'm starting to wonder if this is my fault. She asked me once why people get addicted to drugs, and I said one thing that's common is that people use drugs so that they don't feel things they don't want to feel. I told her it's good when she feels uncomfortable, because she's learning how to feel. She loves playing soccer, but she hates the games, she gets really nervous. I've told her that whenever you get through a game, you're building immunity, you're getting stronger. She's like, "So I don't become a drug addict?" I'm like, oh fuck, this is not what I meant!

"Honey," I say, "I really don't think you're in any danger of becoming a drug addict."

"I'm afraid I'm going to do bad things and then at least you can come find me!" she says.

"Kid, it doesn't work like that. You have control over what you do!"

"What if I go and meet my 'friends' and they hold me down and make me do drugs?"

I realize that she gets freaked out by older kids and what they're doing. And I might have gotten a little too real with her about growing up. She's terrified she's going to hit fourteen and become a different person.

I trust that she's a good kid who is going to be okay. But you better believe I'm reading her text messages to keep tabs on things. That's the one upside to texting: the paper trail. Kids only communicate with their friends by text nowadays, so you don't even have to feel your arm go numb holding the receiver in the kitchen while your kid chats in the other room (talking to you, Mom).

Cell phones are the angel and the devil all at once. They help you stay in communication, and they complicate that communication. Like any powerful tool, a phone must be wielded wisely. We basically need a Rosetta Stone to figure it out. Until then, does anyone know a private eye who can put a tracker on my daughter until she hits twenty? She told me she thinks a third party may be more on the ball than me.

# SIXTEEN

# How to Party as a Parent

**Confession:** *"So . . . are moms still allowed to party or what? I haven't been in a club and barely a bar since my kids were born, and it's depressing to think that's just the reality. I'm still young and fun, WHERE THE PARTY PARENTS AT?!"* –Anonymous

W hen you're a new mom, it's hard not to lose yourself. Suddenly, you have this new baby whose needs you have to put before your own. Keeping this tiny human alive seems more important than cocktail night most weekends —not that you'd even have the energy to get dressed for that. You just want to go to bed and get some goddamn rest.

But as your kids get older and more independent, something interesting happens. For us, it's been like a second teenagehood. With the days of breastfeeding over, I don't have to be shamed by internet moms who say that drinking two sips of pinot is going to, like, poison my milk and turn my baby radioactive. I no longer have to mush up all my kid's food or worry about their bowel movements all the time. It's incredible, the energy and brain space that return after that part is over. Our kids are hanging out with each other or their friends, we trust them to go off without us, and suddenly, we have days when we're feeling the itch to let loose. There's that first time you drink in front of your kids and you realize it's okay, it's pretty normal, actually. So it's like, "We're back, baby! Pour me a glass!"

But then comes the next question. One that maybe most moms don't let themselves think about. How does one party as a parent? We're here to get into it.

Like many things in womanhood and motherhood and parenthood, there are stigmas around moms who drink. Especially in contemporary culture, there are so many gags around "wine moms," which we find quite frustrating. You never see dads getting made fun of for having a beer or a sexy Don Draper scotch. It's expected that men will kick back and enjoy themselves now and then. Yet the wino mother is a much mocked archetype, flattening our legitimate desire to have fun, relax, and enjoy ourselves into this pretty gross parody. We're not for it. This is one of the reasons you have to find your people as a parent.

We've experienced several different kinds of partying in adulthood, and let us tell you, some are better than others. We've put together a little list of these partying experiences so you can have an idea of what to expect when you're reentering the fun-having partying scene, this time about ten years older, but not necessarily wiser.

## PARTY SCENE #1: THE SCHOOL-PARENT PARTY

UPSIDES: For a lot of parents, one of the main hurdles to getting their freak on is finding a peer group for get-togethers in the first place. Maybe you're at a place in life where your closest friends from your twenties have ended up in different cities. Or maybe you're just emerging from the fugue state of young parenthood and are feeling disconnected from other people your own age. For whatever reason it may be, it's not uncommon for parents to feel a lack of community. And while dancing on your own is fun for a while, it can get lonely. That's why a lot of parents hang out with other parents, who they meet through their respective kids, specifically at school. You have commonalities with these people, things to bitch and joke about, and you know you'll be seeing them at school stuff, or even just at pickup and drop-off. And we LOVE low-effort party peers. Find the parent with a kid the same age as yours who sneaks a flask into the kindergarten recital, and you're set for K-6 at least.

DOWNSIDES: You really have to be a good judge of character to know who is going to be down to get down. You suss it out, like going on a blind date. What kind of parent are you? Do you drink wine on the weekends? No? Not our person. Are you inviting us on a weekend camping trip? When we barely know each other? We're not so into adult sleepovers. The main question is, are you on the other side of naughty? Because that's what we're really looking for in a fellow partier. Be careful: If you pick the wrong parent as your party friend, you're not allowed to bring baked goods to the bake sale all of a sudden just because you made a little joke about CBD brownies and the uptight principal. (Actually, a bake sale ban might be an upside.) So TREAD CAREFULLY. Sometimes you have to let the school-party parents reveal themselves of their own free will.

And BEWARE of parent-only school events—that shit is like

suburban Studio 54. Parents who don't get out a lot revert to frat boys and sorority girls, running to the kids' bathrooms to puke out their martinis. Social lubricants let out all the kookiness they've pent up since 1999. These days, the two of us steer clear of these events. You won't remember what you said to someone in the heat of the party, and you certainly don't want it brought up when you have to see them every day at the pickup spot. Oh, if Gossip Girl got her hands on the stories at parent-school functions . . .

## PARTY SCENE #2: KIDS' SPORTS TEAMS

UPSIDES: Similar to meeting parents through school, but with a bit more structure. Here in Canada, hockey culture is alive and well. Hockey, along with some other team sports, comes with a party structure baked into the weekend tournaments. It's possible that the whole point of signing your kid up for hockey is going on weekend trips to Whereverthefuckville and sitting in a hot tub with some beers while your kids run amok in the hotel hallways. The sports team thing is great because there's a mutually agreed-upon idea of what you can do. You're allowed to be drinking together; it's part of the culture. And it's super convenient. You don't have to make plans with your sports-buddy party parents. You know the exact scheduled times you'll be seeing them, and those times already magically work for you and your kids. Having a perma-buddy to sit with in the stands is like having a lunch table crew in high school, complete with protection from annoying people—I'm looking at you, guy who yells at referees during his ten-year-old's house league games.

DOWNSIDES: You actually have to enroll your kids in hockey/ other sports (which is a fucking expensive way to party) and spend your weekends lugging their smelly equipment around from strip-mall-filled city to strip-mall-filled city. And even worse, those hangouts usually die the second your kids are on different teams or your kid decides they now hate whatever athletic activity it is. Not really a way to find a long-term party partner you can rely on to hire a babysitter for a night on the town when you really need it.

## PARTY SCENE #3: ECLECTIC CLUB NIGHT

UPSIDES: Sometimes, you're just craving a club night. We're firm believers in not giving things up just because you're older. A nighttime pool party in Vegas? Yeah, I'm there. And I'm wearing a sexy sparkly bikini. There's no age limit on partying, as far as we're concerned. There was one night in recent memory, after a show we did in Toronto, that was particularly wonderful. With our dancers, our whole team, our husbands, and some other smattering of friends, we went to a bar to go dancing and get bottle service. That's the kind of partying we love—an eclectic group of people, no boring dinner-party talk about where everyone's vacationing or what's going on in the community. Just a total shit show. With bottles, sparkles, chatter, revelry. There's nothing like not being able to hear someone over the bumping music while you dance and ending up in fits of laughter, saying "WHAT?!" only to realize you both just need to go to the bathroom. That's the magic of the club, baby.

DOWNSIDES: Unlike our days of yore, hitting the club every weekend is not really something we have the energy for. The hangover from that night certainly was enough to keep us off clubbing for a while. Plus, the smattering of twentysomethings can kind of lower your vibe and party confidence, and the drinks cost $15, and you'll probably have to ask your kids' university-age math tutor where the cool spot is nowadays (and they probably won't even tell you the *actual* cool spot). And who has the time to do hair and makeup anymore? Clubbing is, like, a whole affair as a parent. You need to be away on a vacation or have a two-day babysitter to make it possible, which, 99 percent of the time, is impossible.

## PARTY SCENE #4: HOUSE PARTY, FAMILY-STYLE

UPSIDES: Like any good party time, whether as a parent or a nonparent, the best nights are the ones that happen spontaneously with people you love. What we love most is being with people who can get down with cocktails and kids running around the backyard screaming. Our ideal night is chaos. Hazy fun, drinking on the back deck with a few couples, a BBQ that turns into an all-night bash. The best nights are the unplanned ones, where the party flows because you're all having so much fun, you just keep ramping it up. No one is dressed up, everyone is relaxed and upbeat, and even the kids get to have a special night. It somehow always ends with some drunk singing, four bags of family-size chips down the hole, and the spilling of some good interparent gossip. These nights make you appreciate a good drink and a round of cards. It may sound lame to nonparents, but it really is the best.

DOWNSIDES: You've gotta have a strong squad that you trust to let the kids roam free while you eat hot dogs and mix too-strong mojitos. We're talking a group chat of people, preferably living within a ten-minute radius, who know what they're in for and love it. This is hard to come by, but once you have it, it's magic. Plus, you might have to explain to your kids why you're leaving your car at your best friend's house and taking an Uber home together. But totally worth it.

CAT

SEVENTEEN

# What
# We Eat
# in a Day

**Confession:** *"I am not a good cook. It's annoying to me that this seems to be a necessary part of being a mom. I don't even really like to cook for myself, let alone an entire group of people. But somehow we have to eat every single day. How is it that motherhood is somehow linked to cooking? Also, am I literally the only mom in the world who is a bad cook??" –Anonymous*

DISCLAIMER: *If you're one of those blessed people who has a partner who spent a semester abroad in Italy and became obsessed with handmade pasta or whose parent taught them the art of high-end homemade cuisine (you know, like meat loaf or whatever) and just loves to cook for everyone without complaint, please skip this chapter and instead use the time to give yourself a little pat on the back for choosing a mate wisely.*

W e've all had that moment, as a mom, when the realization really hits you: For the next decade (at least), I'm going to be responsible for feeding—which encompasses planning, shopping for, preparing, cooking, and cleaning up—an entire family. And yes, of course you can share the load. Your partner maybe will cook once a month and then the meal is revered forever as "Dad's famous pancakes" or whatever. Or maybe your partner will grocery shop, and you pray they know how to interpret "milk" on the grocery list, or else you're having strawberry soy milk in your coffee again. Or you can bribe the kids to clear the table. Isn't it wild how big a job children think setting the table is? And how clearing the table only seems to mean stacking the dirty plates next to the sink? So often, the brunt of the work, especially the organization and the decision-making, falls on mothers.

Anyways, we have to feed them morning, noon, and night until they get to a certain age and can feed themselves, but even then you have to have food available. If a five-year-old wants a piece of toast, you have to toast it. Every time we see glossy food magazines or online accounts with sprawling "easy to do" meal plans for the family, Nat and I have to laugh a little. Like, "Oh yeah, it's so *easy*, just spend six hours every Sunday cutting a thousand vegetables and making three soups, oven roasting, and freezing entrées!" Easy-peasy! And if the kids don't like what you spent hours working on, well, you just didn't do a good enough job. Don't even get me started on the celebrity food diaries that magazines love to publish on Instagram or YouTube. Online cooking culture is fun, for sure. And it can definitely be helpful when you're desperately out of groceries and frantically googling "healthy super-fast recipe using only old canned beans I just found at the back of the pantry." But for us, listening to Kate Hudson talk about her morning celery juice, or hearing how much Miranda Kerr loves to whip up fresh seafood for lunch, or having videos pop up on my YouTube about three easy hacks to make veal parmigiana isn't really so relatable.

Meal planning is one of those things that starts with the best of intentions but rarely ends well. Every quarter of every year, I get the urge to meal plan. I think, Okay, things are really getting out of hand. I'm buying too much food that I end up throwing out because I don't make it, and God forbid anyone else wash and chop vegetables in this house. So I think, It's time, we need some organization. Nat's a master chef, but I can't have her saving my ass every time we have a family get-together. So I'm going to make a meal plan, order the groceries (only what we need for the recipes!), and save money in the process! It's going to be so organized. I'm jotting it all down in my weekly planner. The first week goes great. Week two, not so much. Sunday was hectic with homework and housework and I did not have time to meal prep for the week. Monday, I'm playing catch-up, frantically trying to chop a hundred Brussels sprouts while my kids beg for ice cream (why didn't I buy the slightly more expensive precut sprouts?). I'm convinced that blogger was lying when she said her kids just "gobbled up" her prepared spaghetti squash, because mine hate it. Con artist.

## BREAKFAST

EXPECTATIONS: It's totally reasonable to make custom breakfasts for each kid. Toast with peanut butter and jam, throw a little waffle batter in the waffle maker, use those fresh berries I prewashed last night (victory!), toss a bunch of shit in the blender for a smoothie for my healthy, successful self, and there you go! Fun and easy. I can even be guzzling bottomless coffees from the giant pot I made and half listening to a podcast while making these breakfasts.

REALITY: It's week two of custom breakfasts and the requests are getting to be too much. You want me to make you pancakes on a Wednesday morning? When we have to leave in thirty minutes and you're still in your pajamas? You're dreaming, kid. Turns out this might not be a feasible long-term plan. My mornings are chaotic enough as it is without hosting a continental breakfast like we're the airport Hilton. Time for a rebrand from "custom breakfast" to "custom cereal bar." Just select which one you want, and voilà! Custom breakfast. You can even use the strawberry soy milk your dad bought. And yes, the cereals of choice are Cap'n Crunch and Reese's Puffs. So sue me.

## LUNCH

EXPECTATIONS: As a mom, I'm always trying to encourage my kids to make healthy choices when they eat, and to *want* to eat those healthy choices. Otherwise, they would live on sugar all day long, *Elf*-style, pouring maple syrup into their mouths and sugar into their milk. They'd be thrilled to be Hansel and Gretel. So I pack mega-healthy lunches—turkey sandwiches, leftover pasta in a thermos, a side of baby carrots (please don't expect me to make those bento boxes that are all over Instagram, how can something so cute destroy my will to live?)—and send them off with words of encouragement to actually eat it. When a clean lunch bag comes back home at the end of the day, it's the best feeling. In those moments, it doesn't occur to me that they could have tossed the contents of their lunch containers in the garbage at school. It's a small win, but I need it.

REALITY: This one isn't really about what the kids are eating for lunch, because who knows what kind of lunchroom negotiations they're having. If they're bartering their turkey sandwiches for pizza and Fruit Roll-Ups, more power to them—they probably have a bright future in sales. This is about *my* lunch reality, which does not match my expectation of a kale salad tossed with nuts and a homemade vinaigrette. Inevitably, lunch is literally me cleaning up the things my kids won't eat with my mouth. I'm like a garbage disposal. Scraps of cheese and bread and deli meat, extra chips, whatever. The nubs of chicken fingers have become my favorite thing. I'm an anti-waste icon, is what I'm saying.

And then, after eating the scraps, I'm going for the desserts. The desserts that I told the kids they couldn't eat. I don't want them to see me eating a full box of turtles! Not good for them, but hey, I'm having a long day. Nat tells her kids that the reason she can eat that stuff and they can't is that she's done growing vertically. Genius. No chocolate for you, kid! You need to grow taller, so you need to eat good stuff. But us? We're at max capacity of height here. So yeah, chocolate doesn't affect us.

## SNACKS

EXPECTATIONS: Apple slices, cucumbers with hummus. Hard-boiled eggs. Look at me, cutting up the apples and fanning out the slices. How cute am I?

REALITY: But you know what's easier than buying, washing, chopping, and plating fruit? Goldfish. Nat and I made a rule early on; we drew the line. We say that Goldfish are to adults as dog food is to kids: it's just not food that's meant for us. As an adult, you should not be eating Goldfish. The same goes for those chewy granola bars—that's like a bone for a dog. You can down three of them, *easy*, of course. But that's why it's not for us. That's the debris of childhood, the kind of stuff you find between your car's seat cushions.

**BONUS REALITY**: But then when push comes to shove and it's right in front of you and you're having a bad day, you do eat that stuff. We've all been there.

## DINNER

**EXPECTATIONS**: Chicken breast for the parents, chicken fingers for the kids, some sort of vegetable surprise, and noodles with optional marinara sauce or, if preferred, plain butter and Parmesan cheese. It can easily become a three-course meal with an appetizer of Wheat Thins and a dessert of ice cream bars. Watch out, Barefoot Contessa.

When your kids eat a meal that you made, there must be some psychological thing to it, because it feels like you've just won an award. There's something about feeding your kids and them eating it that just feels so good. And if they happen to say, "Wow, Mom, this is good"? Well, that's better than a Michelin star.

**REALITY**: Shitballs, it's dinnertime again. Haven't looked at a recipe in weeks, kind of forget what a recipe even is. Looks like it's time for macaroni and cheese! Obviously I'm going to be eating it too—I'm hungry! And look at that, now I'm full from the mac 'n' cheese. People tell you as a mom to have an adult meal with your partner, especially if your kids are younger. Eat adult food, have a conversation! Sometimes I envision making an adult dinner and sitting with my husband at the end of the day, but who has the energy for that? When my husband gets home, all I can say is, "I fed your children!" You're on your own buddy, good luck. You're an adult. I didn't sign up to be a cook when I got married! And that, folks, is why God invented restaurants.

## LATE-NIGHT SNACK

EXPECTATIONS: Nothing! Oh, maybe a splash of a vintage wine, but that's just to enjoy while in the bubble bath.

REALITY: The second the kids go to bed? You're eating absolutely everything.

EIGHTEEN

# Sunday Mourning Brunch

**Confession:** *"I remember the days when the weekends used to be for relaxing after a week at work. Now it feels like my weekends just mean that school's out and I'm a full-time mom. I feel like I should be enjoying weekends with my kids and doing all these activities together, like baking cupcakes or going for hikes, but what I'd really like is to have no responsibilities sometimes and spend hours at a boozy brunch."* –Anonymous

It's Saturday morning and I'm taking my kids on errands with me. As I'm trying to parallel park downtown, with a back seat of cranky hungry hooligans and cars honking as I block off traffic, I see these two girls walking by in party dresses, hair disheveled, clutching their Gatorades like a fifth limb. Amid the chaos, I feel so much affection toward these girls, looking like they just stepped out of my past life. When I was in my twenties, hungover, with my hood up and sunglasses on, running to get an iced coffee as big as my head, I dreamed of having a nice house and a partner and a back seat full of kids. I just didn't think about how sleeping in until eleven a.m. as I had that day would be a totally foreign concept to me as a mom.

In my early twenties, I had a group of friends I'd see pretty much every week. Getting together was so easy. Even in an era before group chats, iMessages, and Facebook events, our consistent communication was an IRL group chat. My friends were my family during that time, the constellation I was part of. They were my consistency, and fun was our constant ambition. Thursday to Sunday were essentially designated friend days. We'd hang out nonstop. As I'm dragging my kids around town on a Saturday morning watching twentysomethings deal with the aftermath of their Friday night, I can't help but make a mental comparison between my weekends now and my weekends back then.

## OUR ROARING TWENTIES

**SATURDAY, 5 P.M.** Whatever I've been doing today—lying around my apartment watching TV, out shopping with a friend, going for a walk with no destination in particular, maybe going on a coffee date—is wrapping up. If I was out, I'm returning to my place to start getting ready. A friend is probably on her way over with a bottle of cheap wine or cocktail mix for us to drink while we put on music and do our makeup for several hours, gossiping about who we might see at the bar tonight and what it might *mean* for our evening. Everything simultaneously feels so important and not important at all. Just like last weekend.

## DAYS OF MOTHERHOOD

**SATURDAY, 5 P.M.** The witching hour is upon us. This hour, if not properly watched, can get chaotic. It's reaching evening, and the kids might not have eaten for a few hours, so they are bound to start getting cranky. Which can turn into sibling fights of the most venomous kind—that seem to appear out of thin air, based on nothing. Shit is off the hook at five p.m. My friend calls me and I'm like, Oh my God, doesn't she know five p.m. is the worst hour to be calling me? I don't pick up. But I remember she doesn't have kids, so to her, five p.m. means the start to a lovely evening, not the spooky hour when your kids turn into gremlins. She texts me to ask if I want to get brunch on Sunday, and I haven't seen her in so long I text back *YES!* and put down the phone to try to mellow the kids. I'm going out to dinner with my husband for the first time in months, so I'm all hands on deck trying to calm the kookiness with frozen pizzas (carbs and cheese = happy kids) before the babysitter gets here. I couldn't leave her to sort this all out—who knows if she'd make it out alive.

## OUR ROARING TWENTIES

SATURDAY, 9 P.M. Another girlfriend has come over, and we're all finished doing our makeup. We've tried on at least five outfits each, reassured each other that we look super hot ("No, I promise! Why would I ever lie to you? You look amazing, I'm seriously so jealous of you in that dress. Okay, but maybe try it with different shoes . . ."), and gone through at least two bottles of wine (or tbh, Smirnoff Ice). We're obviously running late for our dinner reservation at the new restaurant that just opened up, but we kind of know one of the waiters, so we're not too worried about it. At dinner, we have cocktails and flirt with the waiter, and it feels like the restaurant didn't even exist before we graced its doors.

## DAYS OF MOTHERHOOD

SATURDAY, 9 P.M. Feet are aching in my shoes. I'm wearing high heels for the first time in what feels like forever. Swelling, more like, probably from drinking one too many glasses of wine with dinner. We're in a cab home, having left the restaurant just when it was starting to get busy and rowdy. I ask my husband why he never reminds me not to order so much cheese and wine together, because now I feel gross and bloated, but we both know if he had, I would've ignored him anyways. I can't wait to get home and go to bed, and I'm praying the babysitter managed to get the kids tucked in. But in my heart of hearts, I know they'll be secretly waiting up until we're home to kiss them good night, and secretly, I love that about them, even if it means I'll get to bed an hour later than I hope.

## OUR ROARING TWENTIES

SATURDAY, 10:30 P.M. We're struggling to decide which bar to go to. Do we want dancing or just drinks? Silly question . . . of course we want dancing. But what kind of music are we feeling tonight? Different crews of people we know will likely be at different places. In the end, we decide to barhop. Once we get to the bar, it's time to ask each other a thousand times the really important, heart-to-heart questions as we survey the dance floor: Are they cute?? Should I go for it?? We bounce opinions back and forth. Thank God we have friends to help suss this out.

## DAYS OF MOTHERHOOD

SATURDAY, 10:30 P.M. I'm sound asleep. Having slight digestive issues, but absolutely passed out.

## OUR ROARING TWENTIES

SUNDAY, 12 A.M. Holding back my friend's hair while she pukes in the club bathroom. Girls keep coming in asking if we need help or water, because the code of conduct in a bar's girls' bathroom is stronger than NATO. One girl even offers us her vanilla body spray to cover up the smell. Once my friend is feeling adequately okay, we send her home in a cab and go back to the dance floor.

## DAYS OF MOTHERHOOD

SUNDAY, 12 A.M. Scrolling through Instagram on the toilet. Damn that cheese plate . . .

## OUR ROARING TWENTIES

SUNDAY, 2 A.M. We don't kiss and tell . . .

## DAYS OF MOTHERHOOD

SUNDAY, 6 A.M. My alarm goes off and I smack my phone, begging it to shut up. I get up to prep breakfasts; my little ones are already awake and wreaking mild havoc. In dire need of coffee, but too lazy to make it, 'cause of course I didn't clean the filter out last night. But if I go to Starbucks I'll have to bring at least one child and purchase at least five cake pops while listening to Kidz Bop the whole way. Not worth it, sigh . . .

## OUR ROARING TWENTIES

**SUNDAY, 6 A.M.** Are you kidding? Obviously I'm dead asleep.

## DAYS OF MOTHERHOOD

**SUNDAY, NOON** I've already had two coffees, breakfast, and a snack—I've been up for so long. I've vacuumed, made a grocery list, hung out with the kids. Now I'm getting dressed for a sacred, special activity: going to brunch. I put on my most comfortable yet chic outfit—athleisure being in style is such a godsend to mothers everywhere. I kiss my husband goodbye and promise I won't be too long (he knows that's a lie), and I can hear the Caesars calling my name.

## OUR ROARING TWENTIES

**SUNDAY, NOON** I wake up to the sound of my phone ringing and stumble out of bed to pick it up. My friend's on the line saying they're going to brunch for mimosas and eggs in half an hour, and to get my butt in gear and meet them there. I say I'm down, obviously, and chug about a liter of water. The hair-of-the-dog trick is sounding good. And so are a ton of hash browns.

—

Brunch, for me and other parents, is symbolic of a different time in our life. It's symbolic of freedom. Of being able to sit and relax for hours and do nothing. You just sit there and eat, maybe have a cocktail. You're even combining two meals into one, how lazy is that? The friend I'm brunching with today isn't a mom. We took different paths, got different rewards, and have had different hardships. I watch her and sometimes I'm just like, "What's it like out there?" I'm rapt by her super-cool life. Just by taking me to this luxurious brunch, she reminds me that there's more to life than kids. As a mom, sometimes it's hard to remember that, or you feel guilty for thinking it. That's why I'm so grateful to her and my other friends who don't have kids—they are such a breath of fresh air. Even though we took different paths, there's space for both of us in this friendship.

There's a part of me that mourns the loss of the things that will never be the way they were when I was carefree in my twenties. The way things are now is hard, and different. Nat and I have given up a lot to raise our children, but we'd be giving up more by not being moms. I take the role of being a mom seriously; it's what I've always wanted. What I mourn is the freedom of making decisions that affect only me. We can't make spontaneous decisions in the same way anymore. But even still, it's not that I want things to go back to how they were. The nostalgia I feel for that time is real, but it's short-lived. When I look around, I see I got what I wanted.

# NINETEEN

# Playdate Anthropology

**Confession:** *"I sort of dread the whole playdate situation. Interacting with my kids' friends' parents who I don't know gives me anxiety. What if they're talking about me and what my house is like? I feel scrutinized, but maybe it's just in my head? How do I handle it when they hear me swear? Or when they learn that I drink at three p.m.?"* –Anonymous

You know the scene. It's pickup time at school. You're standing outside waiting, not looking at your phone because you're trying to do the social media cleanse this week that Oprah said would change your outlook or whatever. It's really testing your endurance, but you're pulling through. You're noticing things you've never seen before—was that tree always there? Is that a new mural? And just when you're contemplating this, a fellow parent walks up to you and says your kids really should get together sometime! You remember why you use your phone so much while waiting for things: to avoid IRL interaction. Now a whole new world has been opened, one that can't really be avoided. Your kid is going over to this person's house for a playdate.

Your relationship with your kid's friend's parent is always an interesting one. Sometimes, if you're like me and Cat, you hope that your kids become friends with *your* friends' kids. In fact, you force it, through constant interaction. But those gosh-darn children had to go out and make friends of their own! With people whose parents we don't even know! And when there are kids going back and forth between different houses, all sorts of dynamics can unfold. Now that we've been through this with several kids, we know this exposure can lead to all kinds of fascinating anthropological revelations, as long as you can survive the awkwardness.

## STAGE 1: THE UNWANTED PARENT-KID MASH-UP

It happens when a parent is feeling lonely and somehow gets a hold of my personal cell number. They text me that they think our kids should get together. I'm not so into matchmaking a friendship for my kid, so I'll take a while to answer. Most of the time I let my kids lead the way if they want to go over to someone's house, especially now that they're a bit older. But then I remember the spectacular physics of playdates: If my kids are at someone else's house, that means they aren't at my house. And if they aren't at my house, I might get one second of alone time! Oh, holy day! So okay, Sandra, yeah, I'll drop my kid off at your house.

Then I make the mistake of walking him to the door—that's such a rookie move. Sandra's like, "Want to come in for a cup of tea and a chat while the boys play?" Well, that defeats the whole point of this playdate! Now, if you offered me a steak and a martini, that'd be another story. But no tea is strong enough to match watching an entire episode of *Bridgerton* in complete, blissful silence. I remember my pro move when I come back to pick up my son: text him when I'm leaving the house so he gets ready for my arrival, and then wait for him in the car outside. None of this *"Ding-dong, let me chat for half an hour at the door while my son melts on the front porch from boredom"* bullshit. We're like spies completing a mission here: we're in, we're out, no questions asked.

And then there's the other side of the coin, when you're hosting a playdate. Pro move here to avoid the pickup chat (which can turn into a very long chat and sometimes passive-aggressive comments about home decor choices) is to get the kid ready when I know their parent is coming. I even tell the kid to wait outside! If they say their parent's not there yet, I just say they're going to be here *really soon* and they're in a big rush so we don't want to hold them up! The worst is when the kid has junk all over the house and is dillydallying about getting it all together. It's like, "Dude, I don't want to sit here talking to your boring parent who's into doing marathons, read the room! Hurry it up!"

## STAGE 2: WHEN "PLAYDATES" TURN INTO "HANGOUTS"

As our kids get to preteen and tween age, playdates change. We're not setting up hangs for our kids anymore: they're texting us asking if it's okay to go to Daisy's house for a few hours after school. It makes me think back to when I was a preteen. I practically *lived* at some of my friends' houses, and my mom never even saw the parents! When you're the kid who's at a friend's house all the time, eventually, the parents just behave like they normally would. You get to know a *lot* about how people live. It can be kind of freaky to send your kids out into an unknown house, but we grill our kids so hard that we tend to feel good about it. Plus, you can often search the parents on Facebook. There have been one or two times where I've sussed out a bad vibe and said to my kid, "You're not going to that house." It's nothing against the kids, of course, but when our kids are spending a lot of time at someone's house, it does have an effect on them. It's all a balancing act in the tween ages.

## STAGE 3: LIFESTYLE RECONNAISSANCE

One of the best things about having your kids go to different friends' houses is that they can become like little spies for you. They're like your eyes and ears, your reconnaissance team. That guy who drops off his kids in the Ferrari—what does his house look like? Or what's the secret that mom with the '90s-era-Tyra-Banks bod is hiding? Well, as soon as your kid goes over to their house for a playdate, all will be revealed. Cat and I love when our kids come home from a new friend's house, because we get to totally grill them. What do the parents do? How long have they been together? What did the house look like? What did you have for dinner? Who cooked it? What kind of soap was in the bathroom? Did they give you soda or strictly water? How stocked is their bar? There's nothing we love more than hearing about other people's lifestyle choices. What's the layout of the houses, how many siblings do the kids have, what's their bedtime, what does their bedroom look like, do they share it? How long are they allowed to be on the computer? It's like the perfect blend of anthropology and gossip. Our kids know by now that when they go over to someone's house, they'd better be prepared to give us the lowdown afterward.

You get exposed to some really interesting ways of parenting, too. Sometimes the kids will come home starving, saying that the only snacks the parents gave them were frozen peas and kale chips. Maybe it's one of those sugar-free families. Everyone is making different choices every day. Which is cool! Good for them! But I mean, would you want to go on vacation with a family who doesn't eat sugar?

Sometimes it's your own kid who shocks you. My son is pretty conservative in terms of his taste. He gets embarrassed by the mere mention of nudity. But the other day, he informs me that his friend's parents have tons of nude figure photos up on the walls, and pictures of the middle finger! He's been going there for years and never mentioned it before. I'm like, what do you think I've been grilling you for? This is the stuff I want to know!

## STAGE 4: SELF-DISCOVERY

After thinking through all this, we realize something. We're on the other end of these imaginary binoculars, too! That same grilling must happen about our houses. Like, I'm pretty sure we're the only moms at school who are verified on TikTok, or who have dildos on their kitchen counter to use as props for work. Compared to us, you, dear reader, do not need to worry about what other parents say about your house. There's no way you have anything weirder going on at your place than we do at ours, and our kids still manage to have social lives.

*We* are the parents your kid's friends' parents are worried about!

CAT

TWENTY

# Not THAT Toy Box!

**Confession:** *"I got a call from my son's teacher that apparently, my son brought–I'm not even joking, I swear–my clitoral vibrator in to school. He had no idea what it was, but I guess he thought it was a cool weird toy?? Apparently he was massaging himself with it . . . mortifying. I keep it in my bedside drawer, never even thought about needing it to be in a more secure place. The teacher was like, "It's not a big deal, none of the kids knew what it was, I just thought you should know," but I'm planning on switching his school and changing my name and never having sex again. AHHHH. I'm too embarrassed to even tell my friends." –Anonymous*

When you're in a business like ours, you get sent free shit. It's one of the great perks of having a social media following. Because of the rowdy nature of our fabulous community of moms, one of the free things we get sent the most of is sex toys. Vibrators, dildos, clitoral stimulators—you name it, we have a shitton of them. We're talking boxes and boxes. The companies all seem to want us to give them an endorsement, but at this point, we honestly have too many toys to even try them all out. But if we did, watch out. We could be the Roger Ebert of the vibrator world. We could make a Rotten Tomatoes but for vibrators. (Do we know any app developers looking for a new gig?) Or maybe it should be market research for our own line of vibrators. Just putting the word out there!

What do we actually do with our surplus of "feminine wellness products"? We bring them on tours with us as props—I mean, they're kind of cute these days, right? Gone are the days of the white, clinical-looking "back massager." Now you have all shapes, textures, and colors available. A silky lime-green pocket rocket? A huge hot-pink dildo? The world's your oyster. Match it to your outfit if you want to.

We're certainly very new to the sex toy world, and also new to talking about it so openly. But it's something that's beginning to get more and more mainstream, isn't it? We see ads for sex toy brands on the side of the road, hear them on the radio. And somehow we've found ourselves smack-dab in the middle of this cultural moment—we're the fairy godmothers of vibrators. We're literally giving them away to our neighbors. Women come to us to spill their sex toy secrets, telling us in hushed tones how they've only ever used an electric toothbrush in the shower. A toothbrush!? Babe, do we have a world of magic to introduce you to. A lot of women say they use it before sex with their husbands. And it's not because sex isn't enjoyable—it's just that sometimes, who knows if you'll get there with him? But this little thing? This is a guarantee. Reviews online will tell you that they "suck the soul out of your clit," and that you'll never want to leave your bed. One woman said she even thinks she blacked out from pleasure. I mean, have you EVER heard a review as good as that for like, an Instant Pot or whatever? THAT'S THE

MIRACLE OF SEX TOYS. It can suck the SOUL out of your CLIT! Who the fuck doesn't want that?!

But given how many of these things are orbiting around us at any given moment, we're bound to have a few mishaps when it comes to kids and their endless curiosity.

Once, when we were on the road, I got a call from my husband. He sounded slightly scandalized, not a normal setting for him. This was one of the first times Nat and I went away, so my husband had his hands full with the kids and was a bit of a solo-parenting novice at that point. Our daughter, he explained, was having a playdate. She was about eight at this time, the age when kids start to get kind of sassy, clever, and snippy; they're figuring out their personality. My daughter and her friend had been quiet for a little while, which wasn't like them.

So, my husband told me, he went upstairs to see what the girls were up to, and they'd gotten into the cabinet under my bathroom sink. There was obviously makeup everywhere, they're eight-year-old girls—okay, fine, that we can deal with. But then he saw that there were sex toys laid out *all over the floor*. And it's not like they were haphazardly tossed out there. No, the girls had organized them, grouped them by color and lined them up from smallest to biggest. Like kids do with Halloween candy so they can take in the magnitude of their haul.

And the girls had no idea what they were! Two little eight-year-olds playing with vibrators like they were Barbie dolls. He's telling me on the phone he doesn't know what to say! How can he tell them to stop playing with them? "Do they know what they are?" he asked me. "Am I going to have to tell the mom when she comes to pick up her daughter from the playdate, 'Hey, by the way, they got into the sex toys'? What the fuck do I say, Catherine?!"

He was spiraling, but I was laughing my ass off. I told him to give the phone to our daughter. I told her that those were work things, and not to touch them. Of course she asked me what they were, and I told her I'd fill her in when I got home. Luckily about three thousand things happened between that phone call and the time I got home, so she forgot all about it. I can't really blame the girls for being interested in the sex toys—why wouldn't they like them? They look like a funky tribe of well-meaning aliens from some cool new Pixar movie.

Flash-forward a few years, and my five-year-old younger daughter walks into my room one day with a clitoral suction vibrator stuck to her face. She said to me, "Mommy, is this a face washer?" I couldn't tell what was more disturbing: that my five-year-old was already aware of fancy skincare tools, or that she had a vibrator stuck to her face. Okay, maybe the vibrator wins that one, because the image is just burned into my brain.

Then, of course, there was the car incident. As you might know, Nat and I often do videos in our cars, so we sometimes have props that aren't typical cargo for a mom's SUV. On this particular day, I had hired the guy who cleans cars at my husband's work to do my car at home, and I had a load of sex toys in my glove compartment. I thought that cleaning the car meant, you know, vacuuming, polishing, whatever—not that someone would be going through the compartments in my car. So obviously, I didn't empty my glove compartment beforehand—and if we're being really honest, even if

I *did* know he'd be going though the car so thoroughly, I probably still wouldn't have remembered they were in there. A dildo here, a dildo there—my brain does not have the capacity to hold on to these kinds of things. It's too busy trying to keep track of my kids.

So anyways, this poor guy cleaning my car found, evidently, my *stash*, and placed them in the garage so he could clean the glove compartment. I guess I had also forgotten to tell my husband that his car guy would be doing my car, so when my husband got home from work, he said to the guy, "Hey! What are you doing here?" And the guy said, "I'm cleaning your wife's car." Then my husband walked into the garage and saw the sex toys all over the place. I didn't have the privilege of watching him react in real time, but he did share some of his lingering thoughts when I got home. Thoughts like, "Are you fucking kidding me right now, Catherine?" And "Now he's going to come into the office and be like, 'This guy's wife is a goddamn horndog that plays with sex toys in the car while at the pickup line!' I mean, why else would someone have sex toys in their car?!" He has a point: our job is kind of unusual, and not easy to explain.

The thing with our kids and sex toys (wow, never thought I'd be writing that phrase in a book) is that they've gotten sort of used to seeing them around. We don't hide much, if you couldn't tell. Because of the nature of our job, our kids are probably more aware of sex toys than most kids are. But to them, they're sort of a funny prop that just goes with all our videos and general silliness. The kids don't really ask specific questions—we are open with them, they know it's a sex toy, but they seem to know enough to know that they don't want to know more than that.

A lot of parts of parenting boil down to this: Maybe there are things you "should" do. Maybe you *should* shut and lock the door when you have sex, or keep your sex toys under a floorboard or something. But then you slip up! You're tired! You're a mom! You've been trying to maintain perfect boundaries all day every day, constantly oscillating between what's appropriate for what age and what you shouldn't tell your kids and what you have to tell them before it's too late—it can all get extremely muddled. It's exhausting. So what happens is that sometimes, something you've been trying to keep secret accidentally gets cracked open. But then it's like, who cares? Why are we making such a big deal out of everything? Call it motherhood and exhaustion, call it laziness, call it whatever you want. We're not claiming our parenting style is for everyone. But sometimes, there's only a certain amount we have the capacity to handle, and only so much we have the energy to keep secret from the kids.

So, if they get into THAT toy box, just know it happens to all of us and there's nothing to be ashamed about. And when in doubt, or even if you just need a laugh, tell them they should ask their dad to explain what the deal is with Mommy's secret toys.

# TWENTY—ONE

# Criminal Minds: The Mommy Files

**Confession:** *"Things have been getting out of hand at my house with my kids lately. They're in this biting phase, and they freak out every time I ask them to do anything. It's getting way too chaotic. Sometimes I have to resort to what feels like criminal behavior just to have one second of peace. I feel like such a bad mom that I can't even control my own kids without bribing them or giving them time-outs." –Anonymous*

There are some parts of parenting that make it feel like a secret society. The kind where you're initiated in a candlelit room by people in hooded cloaks, where things go on that are so perverse, you sometimes feel you couldn't really explain it to people outside the society. Things go awry in families. That's just the truth of it. You're raising small humans who at every second are figuring out how to be in the world, and oftentimes in that process there's clashing, there's personalities causing friction, there's miscommunication that causes heightened emotional responses. And sometimes, your kids are just straight up not behaving!

No one really loves to talk about it, but secretly, we all have our ways of reining in the chaos. You have to! But the ways we do it might not be revered in most parenting books. Most books might tell you some bullshit like you should be meditating with your children, or give you some convoluted theory of how to de-escalate a situation. Which is great. But sometimes your daughter is just being a little drama queen because she's mad her friend got the new doll and she didn't. Or your kid is really pissed off at you for making spaghetti *again*, when they explicitly asked you not to make it. Well sorry, kid, it's been a busy week! Spaghetti is certainly nothing to cry over. And yet here we are, trying to have dinner with a bawling child, tears dripping into the pasta sauce.

The reality is that children act out in all sorts of ways for all sorts of reasons. And of course, tuning in to what your kids are feeling and paying attention to their needs and why they're acting out is totally important. But if you couldn't tell by now, we're here to be real with you. One part of being a mom, especially when you have multiple kids, is just to keep the roller-coaster cart on the tracks. To keep the chaos at bay, the gears grinding smoothly, whatever metaphor you want to use. Just keep everyone moving forward and getting done what they need to get done. This can be completely disrupted when kids take it upon themselves to wreak havoc. Sometimes kids are just being annoying, bitter, frustrated, and there's not anything larger to it. And sometimes you have to resort to what might be described as criminal mommy behavior.

## CAT'S CRIME #1: THREATS

If the universe didn't want me to use threats as a part of my parenting repertoire, then I don't know why it allowed the following events to unfold the way they did. In my head, I've dubbed this event "The Great Basketball Coincidence." So here's the story: A few years ago, we had a family trip planned up north. It was going to be a very sweet cottage vacation that my kids were really looking forward to. We'd been talking about swimming in the lake and barbecues, Dad even volunteered to take them tubing, and we were going to haul our asses to one of those annoying carnivals.

Around this time, in the two weeks leading up to the trip, my two older kids got into some of the most vicious fights I've ever seen them get into. We had recently bought a toy basketball net—you know, the kind that you hang above a doorway. I saw it at Walmart one day and was like, hey, this might encourage a little more physical activity in the winter, get their asses off the couch. They're always asking me what they should do, what games they should play. Here's a perfect thing I can point to—go dribble the tiny basketball! I had no idea what blazing fires this dumb plastic net and ball would ignite.

Like we said, sometimes kids will get into these modes where they start having conflicts that aren't necessarily that meaningful, but are intense nonetheless. My son and daughter started playing basketball, and quickly a competitive side emerged that can only be revealed by the mockery of your flesh and blood. Sibling rivalry is real, folks. There was taunting, there was name-calling, there was a level of attention paid to "the rules" that I'd never seen before. What rules they were playing by is still unclear; pretty sure neither of them know any NBA regulations. The rules were constantly shifting, and they kept screaming for me or my husband to come referee.

It got extremely tiresome, especially when some uncouth bodychecking started. And no matter how many times I tried to resolve this, still they would be name-calling and yelling that the other one was breaking the rules. It was getting down to the last straw. The day they interrupted my monthly leg-and-armpit-shaving shower—which is my SACRED time to light a candle and play some random show I'm not even watching on my iPad that I can't even see through the steam or hear through the streaming water—I'd had ENOUGH. I took the game away for the day, but the rivalry it had stoked was starting to bleed into other parts of the day.

Summer is prime time for fighting. Anything can provoke it. The basketball thing was just a convenient excuse. They also fought about walking beside me. Who got more food. Whose breathing was the most annoying. Just as I was debating how on earth to calm this fight, I got word that our cottage rental had been canceled because of a double-booking. It was clear what I had to do. The universe was giving me incredible ammunition.

The next evening after dinner, another round of the world's most annoying game of basketball was being played in our foyer. I waited for the inevitable screeching.

"MOOOOM," I heard my two whiny children call.

I walked over to them, knowing now was the time.

"Okay, you know what? Since you two seem completely unable to get along for the course of one game, we're canceling the cottage trip. I'm not interested in a family vacation that's full of you two yelling at each other. Trip's off."

Talk about a mic drop.

At first they seemed to think I was just bluffing, which normally, I would have been. But that's why this threat was such a fabulous parenting move. This time, the threat was *real*, and I didn't even have to actually cancel the trip! No money was lost! When the day we were supposed to leave came, they both realized I was serious about not going on the trip. Of course, I didn't tell them I'd rescheduled it for the next month until after they got through at least three games with civility. Maybe I should be selling this idea to the big leagues! Like it or not, threats pay off. Now whenever I make a fake threat, they really buy it. "If you don't stop complaining, we're not going out for dinner tonight." "You know that trip to visit your cousins? If you're going to behave like this, how would you like to be at Grandma's while we're there?" Of course, there's no way I'm leaving for anything like this without one of my kids. But thanks to the Great Basketball Coincidence, I have a much easier time making them believe my threats could be true.

## NAT'S CRIME #2: GUILT-TRIPPING

It's public knowledge that I sometimes suffer from an unknown rash all over my torso. Don't worry, we're trying to figure it out. But it's not such a pretty sight. And lately, my kids have been on a majorly stressful energy wave. We're pretty open in my house, which means I walk around in various half outfits often. I never thought this would offer any parenting advantages, but the other morning,

I was wearing my sports bra when I walked into a scene of my kids bickering over who finished the good cereal. Torso in full view, my children stopped in surprise when they saw me. "Mom! What the hell is on your body!!" My mom instincts immediately perked up. Time to angle this one to my advantage.

"Well, sweeties," I told them, "it's been really stressful in the house lately. You guys are always arguing and fighting, and so the doctor told me it's probably a stress rash." I patted my side and winced for added dramatic effect.

I grabbed my coffee and walked out of the kitchen, leaving them to stew with the knowledge of the *harm* they'd caused. I laughed to myself, congratulating myself on my genius. Might as well get something useful out of this gross rash.

A few days later, I'm surprised and happy to notice that they actually have been better behaved. Then I sort of forget about the whole stress-rash lie—things are busy, time goes by. My rash is starting to go away and I have some cream I'm putting on it. I'm wrapped in a towel, grabbing something from downstairs before a shower, when my son says, "Mom! It looks like your rash is better! Maybe it's because we didn't argue as much today?"

I have to try not to laugh. They must really want this disgusting rash to go away!

I call Cat to relay this information in case she ever needs to use this new strategy. She laughs.

"You know how little kids are always oversharing by accident at school? I wish I could hear the conversations in your youngest's classroom right now. His teacher is probably asking how everyone's weekend was, and he's like, 'My mom got a rash because we fight so much, so now we're trying not to fight!'"

## NAT'S MOM CRIME #3: BRIBERY

We have always been bribers, Cat and I. I have seen Cat bribe in amazing ways. We're very creative about it. This tool is usually the most effective because it *gives* the kids something instead of taking it away. We used to bribe with candy. We had a whole chart system linking good behavior to candy. They never get over candy.

But what's been even more effective recently? Video games. The games that we swore our children would never play are now our greatest tool. Sometimes motherhood is just like that. *Fortnite*, *Roblox*—with these precious tools, we can get them to do anything. Want them to do some chores? Want them to stop kicking and yelling through the biggest fight you've ever seen? If we say, "If you guys stop, at the end of the week you'll get Robux," they immediately drop whatever they're doing, as if we just said a magic spell. "Okay, Mom, sure!" they say. "What time exactly are we going to get it?"

As if you didn't know by now, being a parent is really hard. There's a lot to keep running smoothly, and to us, there's no shame in having some tricks up your sleeve when the going gets tough. You do whatever you can, however you can, even if it's coming up with a white lie in the moment. You know what? You're a mom, you're allowed to do these things. We normalize lying about the Easter Bunny, Santa, the tooth fairy, so let's normalize moms lying, too. And you're also allowed to say to them at some point, "I lied! Yep, I lied." These kinds of lies are genuinely harmless. Don't beat yourself up over them. And if you've never done it? We really encourage you to get it into your routine. It's one of the sacred rights of the Secret Society of Belcaguered Mothers.

TWENTY-TWO

# Apples
# and
# Oranges

CAT

**Confession:** *"I have two kids who have a fairly large age gap between them. Sometimes it feels impossible to keep our family on the same page–the youngest one wants to talk about fairies and coloring books, my oldest is deep into video games and sleepovers with other friends. Am I a bad mom for not being able to make them experience things at the same time, together? Sometimes I feel like the younger one is missing out on his childhood because I just don't have the energy to do the kind of elaborate activities I planned when I was a first-time mom." –Anonymous*

One crisp fall evening, I had just prepared a gorgeous meal for my loving family. Those who know me, and this now includes you, dear reader, know that my preferred method of cooking is cooking by phone. By which I mean, dialing a phone number and having takeout delivered. But Nat, quite the chef, had told me about a dinner she was making that night, and after seeing her brag all over our Instagram, "ladle this and garnish that," I decided that with the extra time I had that night, I'd cook a nice meal instead. I started off by texting Joe, our pizza delivery guy, that I wouldn't be placing an order tonight so he wouldn't think that I was missing and alert the FBI. Two hours later, I'm sitting around the dining table with my family, partway through this rare, elaborately home-cooked meal. I feel like freaking Martha Stewart (post–jail time, of course). It's the time of year when the trees are turning orange and red, and there's a chill in the air that makes you feel so happy to be warm inside with your loved ones. What could be better? I'm doing such a great job at being a mom!

My youngest daughter puts down her fork and lets out a huge sigh.

"Mom," she says, "today at school everyone was talking about how they went apple picking with their families last weekend. Why do we never go apple picking?"

So close! Just when I thought I'd clinched the Mom of the Year award. I look at my other children and silently, with the best of my psychic mom abilities, will them to *not* mention that we went apple picking every year when they were younger.

"Oh yeah," my oldest son says. "I kind of forgot about apple picking. We used to do that every year. That was fun. Then you'd make those apple fritters, remember, Mom?" He says it so casually, not knowing the can of worms he's just opened. In my annoyance, I try to stifle a laugh. I'd almost forgotten that trick I used to pull, where I'd buy a bunch of apple fritters from the bakery and say I'd made them out of the apples we picked. I give my past self a mental high-five. She's a smarty.

As you know by now, Nat and I have seven kids between us. We didn't just pop them out right in a row, you know—it takes time, all that conceiving and birthing and then taking a break to be able to drink and eat fancy cheese again, so obviously there is some age difference between the kids. Between the births of our oldest and our youngest, there was a lot of life to be lived! When you're a first-time young mom, you do something once and it seems fun, and you think, Now *this* is going to be our family tradition. We'll do it every single year, and it will be so special and give our family a sense of history, of security, of magic! We'll go apple picking every fall, cut down our own Christmas tree every winter, make elaborate custom Easter eggs for a huge hunt around the backyard every spring . . . and on it goes, things added to the list every time you do something fun with your first kid.

But then life steps in. Between all the after-school activities, meetings, parent-teacher events, sleepovers, playdates, it feels more and more impossible to arrange for those particular Hallmark moments. Plus, with the older kids, they're a little "been there, done that." They don't care about apple picking so much anymore. And to be quite honest . . . neither do my husband and I. Watching *Moana* all together for the fifth time with a big bowl of popcorn can offer just as much bonding with a *lot* less planning, driving, and gearing up.

My daughter looks at me, mega pissed. "Moooom, you guys all went apple picking without me?!"

"Well, sweetie"—how do I explain this in a way that her sweet little brain understands?—"you weren't born yet when we went apple picking."

"But everyone else went apple picking! That's not fair!"

Ah, there it is. The justice system of a five-year-old. What's fair and what isn't fair—all must be equal in the eyes of a kindergartener. I blame it on the teachers for teaching them to share and be so nice to each other.

But here's the thing: we have to let go of the guilt. When you have more than one kid, it's simply not possible for them all to have the same experiences. It's not reasonable to try to give them the exact same childhood! The conditions are just different. And while my youngest might not get to go apple picking, she *is* going to benefit from the fact that I had two test runs before I got to her! She gets all the rewards of having older siblings, like getting to play with their cool, older friends and listening to Drake on the way to school.

She might grow up a little faster, but she gets the weathered, expert parents we are now instead of the bumbling first-timers we were with her older siblings. She gets to watch movies that we probably would *never* have shown our oldest at her age, like *kissing* movies, but now that our oldest is, well, older, it doesn't feel so wrong. And the conversations you have with your oldest about stuff they're going through doesn't stop just because the youngest can hear. My five-year-old will probably learn about sex and masturbation just because she sneaks down to the kitchen and listens from afar while I'm having a private talk with my oldest. It's like, wait, hey—I didn't mean to tell *you*! But word travels fast under the same roof. You know that saying "A rising tide lifts all boats"? Well, in this case, the rising tide is my kids growing up, and we're all lifted out of the world of Santa and the tooth fairy, and into the world of PG-13, *Fortnite*, and being a bit less precious about childhood traditions.

Plus, youngest kids are pretty much across-the-board more resilient. When Nat's youngest kid broke his leg, the doctor literally told her, "If this was your first child, we'd tell you it'd take a few months to get his leg straight after the cast. But as the fourth child? He should be good in a few weeks."

And while my youngest may not get to go apple picking, between our family and Nat's, she gets to watch six kids go through their tween and teen years before her. That's a lot of role-modeling available!

Of course, I can't tell her any of this. She'll figure it out in time. But right now, her sweet little five-year-old face is totally heartbroken that we went apple picking without her, even though she would probably get bored in a second if we took her, and also she hates apples. Right now, I have to make things right on the apple-picking front.

"You know," I say to her, looking to my other kids and my husband with dagger eyes for backup, "the apple picking isn't really the fun part anyways, honey, it's actually really hard work. It's like being a farmer, you know? It gets pretty boring. And you can get all dirty. What's really fun about it is eating the baked treats after. You know what? I just had an idea. I'll be right back."

I run to my phone and return to my old favorite, my trusty companion, my partner-in-crime—and no, I'm not talking about Nat for once. It's SkipTheDishes, a delivery app. I type in "apple pie" and blessedly, there's some fancy grocery store nearby that happens to have gorgeous-looking apple pies. Twenty-five bucks a pop PLUS delivery, but for my five-year-old to feel like justice had been restored, it's a small price to pay. I walk back to the table and tell her not to worry, we're bringing the best part of apple picking to her. She can probably even eat it on the couch while watching the kissing-filled *Fuller House*. The baby of the family really does get all the special treatment.

TWENTY-THREE

# Dad Crush

**Confession:** *"I hated doing drop-off and pickup for school with my kids for a long time. That all changed, however, when I saw one of the hottie dads who was also on school duty. Now I feel like I'm in middle school. I'm excited to do drop-off and pickup because I might get to see this dad–it's like, I'm not serious about it, I love my husband. But it gives me a little thrill to chat with the dad. My husband's even noticed I've started wearing actual outfits to school instead of sweats. Am I evil/too old to have a crush?" –Anonymous*

F ull disclosure: This is 100% a Nat chapter. While Cat might support me in my pursuit of dad crushes, she herself is not typically one to hop on that bandwagon. But oh baby, I am here to preach the gospel of the dad crush. Not only are you not evil, dear confessor, I think you're GENIUS. I have been known to harbor many a school-time crush in my day, and if you thought that was going to stop just because I got married?! Well, you're a fool. This imagination stops for no one, not even my committed, loving husband.

He is well aware of my fantasies, and he's fine with it. Because I'm amazing, and he knows it's just some harmless fun. Occasionally he'll tell me about a mom he thinks is hot, and I'll be like,

"Yeah, duh, she goes to Spin class every single day and wears a bra. Obviously she's hot. Carry on!" When you're married, people act like you're not supposed to have fantasies or a sexual life independent from your partner. But we aren't actually going to *act* on these thoughts—we're just being honest, because, truly, everybody has these thoughts. It's fun to just let your mind run wild. I am here to tell you folks about the wonders of adult crushing. It's like a school-yard crush, but make it middle-aged. In my books, it's all upsides, no downsides. Let's get into it.

These sorts of fantasies are perfect for where I am in life right now. I've always had a vivid imagination, not even just about love affairs but about future projections in general. It's just fun. Crushes fit right into my wheelhouse at a time when my kids have gotten older. I mean, what else am I going to do? There's a reason shows and movies like *Bridgerton* and *Fifty Shades of Grey* are so popular with our demographic. We're really busy as moms, but we want a little bit of fantasy! So sue us! Watching those shows is a lot less embarrassing than giving your husband your phone to fix the internet connection and him being like, "Were you trying to get onto Pornhub? In the middle of the day?" I'm speaking from experience here, if you can't tell. That's why you never give your husband your phone to fix.

Yes, we LOVE our children and we LOVE our partners and we LOVE our lives and we're so grateful and we do our gratitude journals every morning and thank our lucky stars etc., etc., blah blah blah. But let's be real. Sometimes, the daily grind, the monotony of parenting, the stability we have to create for our kids—it can get boring. It can get so dry, so grueling, that you're praying for something to fall from the sky just to shake it up a little.

And then, something does. Picture it: You've gotten your ass out of bed, packed lunches, wrangled your kids into the car. You're still rubbing the sleep from your eyes at drop-off as your kids hop out of the car when suddenly, you see him. Something jolts through you. It's a feeling you haven't had in years. You spot the elusive, the endangered, the legendary: HOT DAD.

If this happens to you, you've just won the lottery, babe. A hot dad—and keep in mind that when I say "hot dad," I really mean "hot parent of any gender," I don't discriminate when it comes to my crushes; the yoga moms give me the hots too—at your pickup/drop off situation is a godsend. We all need something to occupy our minds during the total drudgery of day-to-day life, and what bends time like a crush? Absolutely nothing. Imagination is God's gift to humans. I always say one of the things that separates us from animals is our ability to get lost in a steamy, dreamy fantasy. So use it!

These crushes are a wonderful way to connect to your school community. Who wants to talk to the other parents about what recipes they've been making or what soccer coach they're pissed at when you could be talking about how hot Daniel's dad is? And wondering what kind of pants he's going to be wearing that day, track pants or slacks?

But as time passed, Daniel's dad and I went our separate ways. Sometimes I still remember him slinging a three-year-old-size backpack over his broad, Patagonia-clad shoulder and smile. Such is the beautiful, ephemeral nature of a pickup/drop-off crush. No strings attached, only fond memories and sexy daydreams.

But no matter—when one dad crush ends, another begins. We've got to keep this entertainment train running. Cat is excellent at helping me spot these crushes. (Cat's husband even sometimes sends me pictures of hot guys he thinks I'd like, and he and my husband are friends!) While she is not one to indulge in my practice, she certainly supports my passion, fueling it with any ideas she can find. Recently Cat told me about a new hot dad at school. Rumor gets around about these things. Apparently, this dad is an actor, which was incredible, because it allowed me to spend the next three hours googling him. What shows he had been on, his star sign, what does he look like without his shirt on, the usual. Seeing this guy at school? Now *that's* what I call motivation.

There's nothing like knowing you're going to chat with the hot dad to kick your ass into waking up a few minutes early so you can put on a swipe of mascara and actually brush your teeth. And if he's an actor? Hell, maybe I'll even put on a shirt that isn't lined with fleece. Dad crushes are even motivational for my children, because my motivation to get out and conquer the day rubs off on them. So take that, parenting books. I know what I'm doing. Let me tell you that when the hottie-with-a-body dad whose parents live on my street comes to visit? It's like I'm suddenly a camp counselor. "ALL RIGHT, EVERYBODY OUTSIDE! It's playtime!" This guy was seriously handsome. The picture of perfection. And then, in a cosmic reward for eating my fruits and veggies and remembering to buy my kid bristol board for his presentation, this dad ended up being a dad at my kid's school. When I tell you he wears clothes like a man in his twenties, I'm not kidding.

In lieu of forcing Cat to tell me about guys she thinks are hot who we actually know in real life, I've taken to making it more abstract, less personal. What celebrity are you into? For me, it's always someone huge and muscly, like the Rock. But for Cat, she couldn't think of anyone for ages. Not one person! Finally, after much prodding, she tells me if she *had* to pick someone, she thinks that the guy who plays Harvey Specter, the lawyer character on the TV show *Suits*, is hot. Amazing choice. A few days later, we go to take our kids to summer camp, and at drop-off, who should we see picking up his children but Harvey Specter! Totally unfair! I've been dreaming about the Rock for years and have never once caught a glimpse. Cat says she's into this Harvey Specter actor *once*, and suddenly we see him every day at camp? We never missed a pickup again, but unfortunately, we did not suavely and sexily get an invite to the set of *Suits*, or even any info on Meghan Markle.

So, have I convinced you yet? Imagination is something we encourage in our kids, it's a great tool for creativity, innovation, yadda yadda. But you know what it's really great for? Getting you through the goddamn day. I encourage you to tap into your middle school boy-/girl-crazy self and go gaga for the parents at school. If you feel like you need permission, this is it. You'll thank me later.

# TWENTY-FOUR

# Welcome to Our Runaway Fantasy

**Confession:** *"Last night I was fully googling plane flights and planning to run away and disappear from my family. I was going to get an Uber in the middle of the night, and no one would be the wiser. I stopped short of entering my credit card info into Expedia. Am I an awful person?"* –Anonymous

There are some days when Real Life feels unbearable. Like, the fact that we have to make dinner every single day for the rest of our lives? Endless loads of laundry that will never go away? Even if I take a vacation, I have to bring my kids, who will for sure cry when there's no chocolate milk at the en-route McDonald's we inevitably stop at?

In order to get through the day, sometimes you need to have an alternate life running in your head. Whenever we're on tour, we always say to the driver, you're taking us to the airport, right? One-way ticket? It's not that you don't love your life . . . but it can be good to have a fantasy to dip into to calm you down, remind you how fabulous life can be. Especially when you have sixteen errands to run, taxes to file, a kid pissed off with you, a partner stuck late at work, and no groceries. We have dozens, maybe hundreds, of these fantasies and daydreams. They're playing on the Netflix in our minds at all times. How do you think *Fifty Shades of Grey* made all that money? To encourage you to try this out, we present to you our tried-and-true favorite runaway fantasy. Feel free to use it.

It starts like this. You come home and there's a car waiting for you. Sleek and chic, and a handsome chauffeur is opening the door. He says, "Everything's taken care of, miss. Food is made for your kids, there's a bag packed in the back seat and it contains all the cute things that you've added to your online cart but never bought. There is a bougie carrier holding perfectly sized mini toiletries instead of one Herbal Essences shampoo wrapped in a plastic bag. We're taking you away somewhere hot for a few days. There's a doctor on call for your family, a lawyer in the wings in case shit hits the fan. Your children are going to be perfectly behaved, and the person who's watching them is even better than Mary Poppins. No one is going to barf or lose a tooth or hurt themselves, it's guaranteed. And you won't need to feel guilty, because they're going to have so much fun, so much entertainment, they won't even miss you! They won't even try to contact you!"

So you say, okay . . . and you get in. Your best friend is waiting for you in the back seat, and her kids are also being watched by an all-knowing Mary Poppins type. Your drive to the airport is traffic-free, and you don't even get carsick. At the airport, they don't make you take your shoes off at security, like you're a PRINCESS or something, and you even get into one of those airline lounges that you've tried to sneak into for the past two decades. Inside, you steal a dozen cookies and three magazines.

On the plane, you get a mimosa and one of Oprah's book picks of the year. You're in a matching fashionable-yet-comfortable travel set instead of your usual leggings, sports bra, and university hoodie. No one asks you to put Liza Koshy vlogs on the TV.

You smash cut to some tropical place, somewhere hot. There are no line-ups, and there are endless cocktails. But these cocktails are special—they don't give you a hangover.

Your best friends are all there, the ones you haven't called in two months but do truly love, the childless ones you envy on Instagram, the high school old faithfuls, all by the pool. There's bottle service and unlimited gorgeous food, there's dancing. You're wearing all the new cute trends that you've wanted to buy but didn't. You have on stilettos, and they don't hurt your feet; you can't trip in them, either. You're dancing to your favorite songs; it's like the DJ is predicting your needs.

Dinner is fabulous; you can eat and eat, even a whole cheese plate, and never get full or bloated. You arrive at your room, drunk and happy.

But then, suddenly, a thought. Whatever happened to your husband?! Did someone kill him to make this all possible? Just when you're about to put out an Amber Alert for him, he appears at the door. He's showered, shaved, and is dressed like he's going to work instead of going to the store with you in sweat shorts. And because everything is perfect, you want to have 24/7 sex. No morning breath, no complications, constant orgasms. He'll even roleplay *Outlander,* like you always wanted. Post-lovemaking, your husband retreats to his own separate room far away, only meeting when it is convenient for your schedule. You get an email update with a photo of your kids all smiling, teeth brushed, in matching outfits at a pottery class. No one expects you to come back ANY time soon.

You sleep in for the first time since a baby came out of your vagina, knowing you have a spa day booked for the next morning.

Sigh. That's one of our recent favorites. Go ahead, reread it. Live in it a little longer. Come back to it whenever you need to. Then, on to reality . . .

We, as parents, all need an escape. While fantasy getaways with omnipresent car drivers who pack perfect luggage aren't possible unless you're Kim Kardashian, little respites like the occasional daydream about Henry Cavill, or reading a trashy romance novel, or sitting in your car for just ten minutes in silence even if it means being the last one to pick up your kid from soccer practice, are beyond okay. The fact is, you cannot keep up with this crazy life of juggling it all without thinking about disappearing from it every once in a while. We will not mom-shame or parent-shame for this! Daydream away, comrades! Guilt-free! We'll see you on the mind-beach—we can have a cocktail and talk about our kids.

# TWENTY-FIVE

# Taking Back Our Time

**Confession:** *"My biggest guilty pleasure is booking an extra day on the end of a business trip where I'm not working, just staying in my hotel room, ordering room service, watching bad cable TV, and just being ALONE FOR ONCE. Or maybe I'll even go to the hotel bar and fantasize about having a one-night stand. But every time I do this, I feel so guilty!! I feel like I'm a horrible mom for not wanting to rush back to my kids as soon as possible." –Anonymous*

It's been one of those weeks that make you wish you were a vampire. You know, so you'd never have to sleep. After a twelve-hour day of parenting, you could actually have a moment to just decompress, rather than immediately crashing into bed the second you finish cleaning the kitchen (for what feels like the tenth time that day). It's the kind of week when I haven't even looked in the mirror for two days, hair be damned, the kind of week when I go on Instagram for a second and I'm shocked that the outside world still exists. This morning I check my calendar and see that it's only *Wednesday* and internally scream. My son comes running from the next room—oh, whoops, maybe that was an out-loud scream.

"Mom, are you good to take me to hockey practice tonight?" he asks.

I almost clamp my mouth shut to not scream again. When will it ever end?!

"Sure, babe."

After I drop my kids off at school, I head back to the empty house and sigh onto the couch. The fact that I have to do a workday and then pick up the kids, make them dinner, take them to their extracurriculars, get them ready for bed, put them to bed . . . that's like eight more hours of mom time and I don't know if I can take it. Some days, I'm so busy and burnt out that my sense of self is confusing. Like, who even am I if I'm not a woman trying to remember what kind of yogurt flavor my kids prefer? I haven't even thought about what kind of yogurt *I* like in months. There's only one solution for this self-slippage, this deep, dark, I-can't-fathom-wearing-anything-but-sweatpants-for-the-rest-of-my-life kind of fatigue. I call Nat. She picks up on the second ring.

"Okay. Code Red. Emergency," I say, which of course doesn't faze her in the slightest.

"What's up this time?"

"I'm looking at myself in the mirror right now and I'm like . . . who is this woman before me? Who is this woman who has a coffee stain on the shirt she's been wearing for three days? Who is this woman whose hair is defying gravity? And I can't gather the energy to change or brush my hair. I used to have fun, right? Hey, do you know what kind of yogurt I like?"

Nat starts to laugh.

"Girl, my God, if I have to pack one more frickin' lunch . . . I'm going to sue whoever invented packed lunch. What happened to all those school cafeterias serving sloppy joes that they show in nineties TV?"

"Nat, I feel the dire need to escape right now. Is that horrible?" I ask.

"No way. Let's do it."

"What, just like hop on a plane?"

"We could *Thelma and Louise* it, minus driving off the cliff?" she says.

"I call dibs on Brad Pitt."

"I'm thinking more like, what if we ditch our families this evening and go get drinks downtown?"

THIS, ladies and gentlemen, is why you have a best friend. God, have I ever told Nat what a complete genius she is?

"You are my soul mate," I respond.

"Like I didn't know that. Look, let's see if we can call the grandmas in for some quality time with the grandkids tonight and book it to a bar. Preferably one known for strong cocktails and an average age of over twenty-five."

Five hours later, it's four p.m. and we're sitting across from each other in a booth, grinning like we just pulled off the greatest heist of all time. We're *Ocean's 8* up in here. My hair is actually looking *wonderful*, I've put on jeans, which feels like a small miracle, and our waiter is arriving with our drinks. I smile at Nat and feel tension leave my body. I'm a human again.

After catching up on the only topics we can think of that don't involve our kids (sexiest Netflix shows, vague world news based on Tweets we've read, whether I want to try the DivaCup and if so, do I order a large?), I start to feel a creeping sense of dread. I try to ignore it, but it's hard. Nat reads my mind.

"Cat," she says to me after we order another drink, "do you feel a bit guilty right now?"

"I was just thinking that and trying to get it out of my brain! It's like, sheesh, can I just have one fucking evening without feeling shitty about mom responsibilities?" I respond.

"What do you think our families would think if they knew this is where we were right now? That we just aborted mom duties and called our moms in so we could get shit-faced downtown?"

I sigh.

"They'd be like, 'Okay, thanks, Mom, you don't love me enough to come put me to bed?' Every time we leave they say, 'Oh, you're leaving *again*?' It's like, what do you mean, 'again'?! I haven't left your side in days! 'Oh, you're not watching me play soccer *again*?' I've missed like two games in your whole soccer career! I even signed up to be snack mom TWICE this season, TWICE!"

"Completely," Nat agrees. "They have this unbelievable ability to make us feel crazy for spending any money on ourselves, or time on ourselves."

"You know, we haven't done this in ages, but when we used to do day dates, we'd get a babysitter to come over during the day, and I felt like I was going to get arrested! Just for leaving the kids at home when I *could* have been spending time with them."

"It feels so foreign," Nat says, "to do things you're not 'supposed' to do. Like what we're doing now."

Why is it that as moms, we feel guilty for taking time for ourselves? Why does it feel like a selfish thing to be doing?

Well, we know why, actually. It's hundreds of years of patriarchy that's led us to believe a mother should put her children's needs before her own 100% of the time. That once you become a mother, you forfeit your right as an autonomous person to have desires and needs and independence. Of course, as parents, we will always be there for our kids. But why do our husbands not face the same guilt when they stay out? Even in a contemporary context, when the people in our lives seem to believe that gender equality should exist, these outdated gender roles still manifest in our daily lives.

While we're discussing this, a big group of people dressed in suits and formalwear sit down at the table next to us. It's clear that they work together. It reminds me of an unfortunate truth both Nat and I know: Our husbands do this kind of thing all the time—go out for drinks with clients or coworkers. To "team-build," schmooze, whatever. They're "working" at the baseball game, at the steak house, at the golf course. We have a lot of female friends who work downtown, and it's the same thing with them. We're here agonizing over our guilt about being away from our kids, but if these cocktails came under the guise of work, there'd be no judgment attached. These professional women certainly face these challenges as well, especially if they're mothers, but there's something about the excuse of work that makes this kind of socializing more permissible. It's why Nat and I have sometimes rented a hotel room downtown to make videos or livestream from. We just want a break, and it seems like using work as an excuse is the only way we can do it without feeling guilty!

We even receive flak sometimes when we go away on our tours. Moms at the grocery store, or online, wherever, will tell us they can't *believe* we're going away, that they couldn't *imagine* being away from their kids for so long. How do we do it? They're not overtly calling us bad moms, but their condescending tone surely conveys the message. And why do they do this? It's called internalized misogyny, honey!

We feel so much guilt for having adventures that don't include our families. For taking time for ourselves, even if it's just one single evening off when the rest of the week, we're bending over backward organizing everything for our husband and kids. That kind of guilt has been culturally instilled in us, definitely. It's why our kids don't freak out when Dad doesn't come home until late, but God forbid Mom stays out for a few extra hours. And the cultural scrutiny is so strong that even when no one knows we're spending time away from our families, we still feel the eyes on us. Like some sort of all-seeing mom-guilt police.

It even feels like my husband and my nanny are the mom-guilt police. The other day I was lying down cuddling my daughter. She got up to do something and I stayed there on the sofa looking at my phone. I heard someone coming up the stairs and I JUMPED up to pretend I was doing something. If I hear my husband in the driveway, I feel that immediate stomach drop like I need to be busy when he gets inside. God forbid a mom should be sitting down just having a moment.

"You know what I think?" Nat says after we've shared a look about the group of businesspeople next to us. "I think that it's a woman's responsibility, a caretaker and parent's responsibility, to take back their time. We have to debunk this myth that women, parents, are evil for taking time to indulge in fun or pleasure."

"You're totally right," I say. "You know, this guilt is something we contribute to as well. By not leaving, by always being there, by not taking time for ourselves, we're part of the problem too. We let them rely on us one hundred percent of the time, and so they expect us to be there one hundred percent of the time."

"Remember when we were doing the podcast a few weeks ago?" Nat laughs. "I'll never forget this. We were away for an hour or two recording, I come home, and no one has eaten! Not one kid. Daddy was home but didn't make them lunch, and everyone was waiting for me to figure out what to eat. It's like, you guys know how to open a fridge! What the fuck has happened to our lives that our children—who are like, not tiny babies, they are preteens—aren't feeding themselves when they're hungry? It's like we're in a bad relationship, getting walked all over all the time, and we complain about it but do nothing about it. You're too tired to change it, and you're caught in an exhausting loop of shoulds and shouldn'ts."

I feel a revelation coming on. We're onto something here.

"Nat, that's exactly it. What has happened to our lives, our families' lives? We have to take more time to ourselves, but it's also a two-way street. It's a habit, a practice, and it's something that will also benefit our kids. We have to set the expectations and the boundaries so that we have independence and so do they. We're still a family unit, but we all need a little room to breathe, to do things on our own, especially now that they're getting older. It's a normal part of life, it's a wave they know how to ride, when we take the night for ourselves."

So we make a pact, then and there, several cocktails in: We will set boundaries and expectations with our families that it's normal, healthy, and expected that Mom has time for herself now and then when she needs it. No questions asked. We deserve downtime too. And it benefits everyone: the more responsibility we allow other members of the house to have, the more capable they all become, partners and kids both.

Sometimes when we're in the thick of being moms and not doing things for ourselves, we feel so boring. The fuel within us is gone, the independence, the giggles and laughs, it's all gone because we don't feel recharged. When you find a little piece of the world for yourself, whether it's taking a break to go to some cultural event alone, or having a girls' weekend, or seeing your parents and siblings without your partner and kids, it feels invigorating and necessary because it is! It's necessary to remind yourself of who you are outside of being a wife and mother. And then, in turn, when you're more recharged, you can be a better wife and mother. There were things you loved to do before you had kids. You don't just love being a mom. You have to find what that moment is and take it, because no one is going to give it to you; no one, nobody, is going to say you need a break.

I think about my daughter. I wouldn't want her to think you have to give up independence and alone time to be a mom. That cements it for me.

When I get home that night, it's nine, the after-school chores have all been done and I go to kiss my kids good night. All of them ask me where was I, why wasn't I home to make dinner, why didn't I watch them play soccer or help with their homework. To each of them I say, "Sweetie, I love you, and I hope you had a good time with your grandma. Tomorrow, we're going to have a little talk, and I'll explain it all to you. Trust me, it's for a good reason."

And then I half watch *The Vampire Diaries*, which my daughter left playing on the TV downstairs, while packing lunches for the next day. I realize I never wanted more time in the day—no amount of time would make me feel like I was doing enough. I just want boundaries, and the permission to take time for myself. And besides, those vampires all have those horrible dark circles under their eyes from not sleeping—and I don't have the time or energy to add another step to my makeup routine.

# TWENTY-SIX

# Letter to Our Younger Selves

**Confession:** *"You guys are cool and seem to always be having so much fun. You give me hope for when I'm a mom. What advice would you give your younger selves if you could speak to them, knowing what you do now?"*
–Anonymous

*Dear Younger Cat and Nat,*

*You're a lot like the young people we hear from who aren't parents yet. They want to have kids but are terrified of what will become of their identities and their passions. They want to know what they'll be in for as parents. We've learned a lot of lessons along our journey as mothers, and there are a few things we wish we had known as we walked our path. And so we are scribing this letter to you, young, naive, and, above all, majorly hot Cat and Nat of the past. And also to all our anxious young readers teetering on the precipice of parenthood—we see you and we love you! (You are all also majorly hot.)*

*First of all, there are the expectations of motherhood that you've absorbed, and then there's the reality. This is a huge, overarching theme of almost everything we talk about. When you're younger, your image of being a mother is based on images from TV, rom-coms, Hallmark cards. Those images of a family all in matching outfits on a white sandy beach.*

*You think, That's what I want. That calm, serene, playful family. I want to be at the pumpkin patch and make all these beautiful memories.*

When you get to that pumpkin patch or sandy beach in real life, wrangling all your kids and wiping snot off everything, it doesn't exactly feel like what you imagined. A lot of moms get overwhelmed with the imperfection of life. Expectations come crashing down around us, and it can feel totally rotten. It will go wrong, young Cat and Nat, that we can guarantee. It will not be all smooth, Gap-catalog-family frolicking. Your kids might fight all day during the time you were hoping to get a perfect picture of everyone having fun. But it's not about the picture. There might be only thirty seconds in a day when your kids are getting along with each other and with you. But in that thirty seconds, God, they're so cute! They have each other's backs, they're laughing, and it's perfect, in its own fucked-up way. And I know you probably hear this all the time and roll your eyes, but it really makes it all worth it.

To the young versions of ourselves, stop comparing yourself to your expectations and be okay with what and where you are. You don't have to aspire, you just have to be. Parenting is a long-term journey. It's not about those small magic moments we try to orchestrate to impress some all-seeing judgment board. The only reason the picture-perfect-white-teeth clan is your ideal version of a family is that it's the only example you've been given. But now it's time for new examples.

Forget the rom-coms. If anything, the reality of family life lies closer to a sitcom. Parents always arguing, there's always a problem, it's a shitshow everywhere. Those who find comedy in life are the real winners. That's way more real. You have to laugh at some of the things we go through. Like they say, if you're not laughing, you're crying.

## CAT

*Take Christmas, for example. More often than not, Christmas will be a bust! The kids will get overtired, they're ungrateful, there's too much stimulation, they wake up at four a.m. so by noon, the novelty of their presents has already worn off and you're left with tired children AND parents. It's the random moments that make the best memories—like when you sit down and play a game together for forty minutes on a Wednesday when you haven't all been together in a week. In those moments you get the undivided attention and conversation that gets missed during all the hype of a "special" day.*

*We have to stop acting like it's our responsibility to make everything perfect, and start enjoying moments as they come, whether you have kids or not—that's something I wish I'd embraced before becoming a parent. Parenting is kind of like New Year's Eve. You wait and wait and wait, the baby finally comes, and you're expecting this magic moment. Sorry to tell you, young Cat and Nat, but for us, there was no magic moment. I'm wearing a diaper, my vagina hurts, I've got stitches, this thing is crying and it's not even that cute yet. I thought it would be cuter! And that sets the tone for motherhood—there are so many uncute moments. Life is about the moments that sneak up on you, like a party that you never expected to be so fun, or like when you unexpectedly meet your life partner. Let go of what you think should be happening and when it should happen, and live in what it* is.

## NAT

*And speaking of life partners, your relationship with your partner is going to change when you have kids. It just will. Not necessarily for the worse, not necessarily for the better. It will just be different. I thought that when I got married and had kids, my relationship would be naturally strong, because we're both parents and we share this kid, our lives, house, money, everything. But it becomes complicated. It's not the relationship you married into. Often, your partner comes from a different upbringing than you—different lifestyle, different parenting techniques. Cat and I always say that it's like all of a sudden, you're living with a stranger whom you're raising kids with. But you have to come together as a united front when parenting, or else it can be majorly confusing for the kids. Sometimes, you have to sit there and think, Well, I would never have said or done that, but we're a team, so I have to back them up. Get ready for that with your chosen partner, and don't sweat the small things. Except probably get on the same page about some of the big things, like the kid's name.*

## CAT

*Things will bother you that never used to bother you. A friend of ours just had her first baby, and when it's a brand-new baby, it can't really do anything. Her husband went out and got totally shit-faced on New Year's Eve and came home and slept in the basement. Before the kid, our friend wouldn't have given a fuck about this. But because the baby is there, she's furious that her partner is sleeping while the baby is awake. I relate to this so much. You don't even need anything from the partner, the baby can't do anything! You're just putting it on your boob or a bottle in its mouth! But still, if your partner isn't there to help, it's like, "I want to kill you right now!" That's how relationships change as parents. It's a weird thing. There are a lot of confusing feelings.*

*You're thinking, Whatever, it won't happen to me. Sorry, young Cat, but it will. I know where you're at right now. You're sitting at a stoplight thinking you'll never stop holding hands, you'll never not make out at a stoplight, even when you're married. Fast-forward: Your husband is eating popcorn and you could murder him because of how loud he's chewing. It's not bad and it's not good, it's just a weird evolution of intimacy. And it's your story, and you're writing it every day, and that's real romance.*

## NAT

*It's also important to remember that you can be a mom and love your life, but also sometimes hate your life. You can be a mom and still be lonely. You don't see your friends as much anymore, and that's why we've found it really important to have someone you can be fully vulnerable with and create a strong friendship with outside your home. When you have a mom friend, you can beat the shit out of a topic with them and they're there with you, whereas your partner will probably try to fix it. Which is sweet, but not the point sometimes. Plus, there are days when you're going to hate your partner. Like, not actually hate them, but hate them for that day. You're going to need to say to your friend, "I hate my partner, I hate my life!" And you don't mean that. I mean, you do, but you don't. You need a friend who knows you're just having a hard day and won't bring out the divorce papers. Who can handle your crazy, who is down for you to drop off your kid at their house when you're having a moment, and who won't think you're going through a "really hard time" when you do that—you're just having a day. If someone is looking to make a huge deal out of these normal moments of life, that's someone who is just looking for drama. That's not the kind of friend you want by your side.*

## CAT

*And to that point, if you think your life is a dirty little secret, it's not. You're not the only one dropping your kids off at your friend's house because you just can't deal. Yes, maybe you've given your kids butter noodles and salt for the fifteenth day, or you did their project for them instead of teaching them how to do it because you just need this Sunday night to be over. You might question every single thing you've done, but you need to know, younger us, that you're not alone. You're expected to do it all, and you just can't!*

## NAT

*There are so many different ways to parent. When I was young, young Nat, I thought there was just one way. I thought "mom" was the category. Then you have a baby and start hearing about all these different styles of parenting, and there's judgment about them all. But the judgment doesn't matter—that's what you need to remember. People judge because they feel insecure about what they're doing. If someone thinks sleep training your kid is horrible, they have to think that way because they didn't sleep train theirs. You judge people for doing things differently than you—that is, until you mature. Until you meet a lot of moms and* realize that they all parent differently and they're all amazing moms. We've met so many fantastic moms on social media and on our tours, and ultimately, we're all doing the best we can. No matter what. So though we may look, sound, and parent differently, we all have the same core want for our children to be happy and looked after, no matter what.

## CAT

Plus, even if you do mess up, those failures are what make resilient people and resilient families. If your kids feel loved, they won't care that they're not all in matching sweaters, or that you're wearing the same yoga pants every day for a week without actually doing any yoga. That stuff doesn't matter. To my younger self, just chill out. For your first baby, you're mashing up organic avocado, and guess what? By age six, they're mowing on a chicken nugget and french fries and their newborn sibling without any teeth is trying to gnaw on a nugget too. It's fine. (Once we were in a hockey rink, and we looked over and Nat's youngest kid was barefoot, eating gum off a chair. He's still alive!) You're going to go through stuff. Your kid bleeding from the head and needing stitches, a broken leg, all-night barfing. You will curse yourself for not preventing it. But it's okay. You're overcoming a challenge together. These really hard things make you stronger as a mom, and they make your kids stronger too. It's all part of the experiment of life.

## NAT

And yeah, it's really annoying that this is such a fucking hard job and no one will ever give you credit for it. If women don't have other jobs, they *sort of whisper, "Oh, I'm just a mom." But that's the biggest* just *in the world. Even moms who say they're bad moms, look at what they do in a day. It's impossible that that shit actually happens! We hold ourselves to the highest standard. We take our kids to appointments, keep their teeth in their mouths, teach them about life, make all the fictitious holiday characters become real, and make meals every day on top of that? The average mom is a fucking superhero if you really break it down. But we put no value on this. Why? It's an invisible part of society, the way moms keep the world turning. Moms do it without the accolades, without the acknowledgment.*

## CAT

*That's why when you're a mom, you need yourself more than ever. No one is telling you you're a great mom all the time. You're sitting in this journey by yourself. That's why women need each other. The only person who can relate to this is another mother. You're going to fail daily. You're going to* feel *like you're failing daily. But you're not actually failing. It's not being a bad mom, it's called life!*

## NAT

*My younger self imagined a very specific future. I would see people and think,* That's *what I want my life to be like. I vision-boarded for it even before Pinterest was invented. I was sure it was going to feel a certain way. And that it would be enough, that it would fill my buckets, and I wouldn't need to worry about myself anymore because I would be so involved in being a mother that all the other parts of myself would just fall into place. What I didn't think about is that there's still so much life outside my kids. My kids will always have an impact on everything I do, but just because I got married and had children doesn't mean I'm just a wife and mother. Before, I thought I would just focus on those around me and that would be my identity. Now I realize it's so important to keep who I am and keep doing the things I like to do, to follow my own dreams too. Because that will affect my kids and set a good example for them, but it will also recharge me and make me a better mother. Being yourself and following your dreams is exactly what your kids need to see.*

*No matter how wild or weird you think your confessions are, or how badly you feel you've screwed up, trust us, there are loads of parents out there feeling and doing the exact same thing. If anyone knows that, it's us. Parenting is a bumpy ride, a wild ride, and a totally annoying ride. But it's your ride, and it's your kids in the back seat. Your job is to launch your kids into the world and give them all the love you can. Besides that, just make sure you don't do anything we wouldn't do. Which, as you know by now, means you should rule out absolutely nothing.*

*Love Always,*
*Cat & Nat*

# Acknowledgments

Now that everything's on the table and all the secrets are published for the world to see, we want to give our gratitude and thanks to all the moms who shared their confessions with us and ignited the conversations for this book. And thank you to all of you, our readers, who will keep our confessions between us 😊.

Thank you to our editors, Donna Loffredo and Rachel Brown, for understanding us and helping us put our stories into the world. As in everything we do, thank you to our kids and husbands for being their wild, wonderful selves so that we have endless content to share with you all. Oh, and supporting and loving us, too.

# ABOUT THE AUTHORS

CATHERINE BELKNAP and NATALIE TELFER have been friends since they were teens, but grew closer with motherhood when they chose to confide in each other about the more taboo topics of parenting. It wasn't long after that when they decided to bring the conversation online in hopes of helping other moms feel less isolated. Their rapidly exploding community of like-minded moms tune in every day to watch them rewrite the paradigm of the "perfect mom."

Also by bestselling authors
# CATHERINE BELKNAP
## and NATALIE TELFER

"*Cat and Nat's Mom Truths* takes everything that's scary about being a mom and makes it hilarious."
—**KAREN ALPERT**, *New York Times* bestselling author of *I Heart My Little A-Holes*

RODALE
BOOKS

Available wherever books are sold